RECYCLE

Moira & Nicholas Hankinson left London behind and with it careers in design and the art world. Their first staging post was Somerset, where they designed and produced an internationally acclaimed range of furniture and accessories for the house and garden. Passionate about their subject, they are acknowledged as early exponents of reclamation, using recycled timber, glass and ironwork in many of their creations. Their homes have been restored using recycled materials whenever possible and have featured in interiors magazines. With a wealth of experience and now settled in Herefordshire, they continue to run their company, Brainge Ltd, specialising in sympathetic restoration of neglected houses. They are the authors of a number of books and have appeared on television showing their design ideas.

RECYCLE

Make your own eco-friendly creative designs –
over 60 projects for home & garden

Moira & Nicholas Hankinson

KYLE CATHIE LIMITED

To Antonie Mouthaan

First published in Great Britain in 2006 by
Kyle Cathie Limited
122 Arlington Road
London NW1 7HP
general.enquiries@kyle-cathie.com
www.kylecathie.com

ISBN (10-digit) 1 85626 681 8
ISBN (13-digit) 978 1 85626 681 9

Previously published in Great Britain as *Salvage Style in your Home* and
Salvage Style in your Garden and in the United States as *Salvage Style in
your Home* and *Salvage Style for Outdoor Living* in 2000 and 2001
respectively.

Text and designs © 2000, 2001, 2006 **Moira & Nicholas Hankinson**
Photography © **Tim Winter** except those listed below

Senior editor: **Helen Woodhall**
Designer: **Kevin Knight**

Colour repro, printing and binding by Colourscan, Singapore
Printed and bound in China by SNP Leefung Printers Ltd

PICTURE ACKNOWLEDGEMENTS
8 centre right, 12 centre right, 37 right, 245 bottom Bob Whitfield; 36 Paul
Anderson; 98 top left and right Madeleine Boulesteix; 124 left, 150, 155
bottom left, 168, 173, 177, 181, 182, 185, 196, 222, 241, 247 bottom, 248,
Moira and Nicholas Hankinson

Contents

An old Gothic-pattern painted iron bench and an occasionally-used iron garden roller nestle below an ivy-clad stone wall and a disused telephone box once installed in the nearby village.

INTRODUCTION

Recycling is newsworthy. Scarcely a day passes without some mention of the need to reduce, reuse and recycle. Open a newspaper or switch on the television and the headlines flash before us: 'Great ways to go green', 'Reduce waste, help save the planet', 'Pick of the best recycled products' and 'How eco-friendly are you?'

Historically, many materials thought to be past their best were routinely recycled. In medieval times, stone and timbers from dilapidated cottages or houses were salvaged and reused to build new dwellings.

The late nineteenth and early twentieth centuries saw gypsies, scrap-metal dealers and the rag-and-bone man all making a living from collecting cast-offs, and selling them on for recycling.

NEAR RIGHT

Open the skilfully painted double doors of this floor-to-ceiling cupboard bought at a flea market and you will find an array of compartments comprising shelves, drawers, hooks, as well as a fold-down table top with a perforated zinc cupboard above, which suggests it may have been used for food storage at some stage.

CENTRE RIGHT

An imaginative use of reclaimed materials can be seen in Hank and Sophia Terry's exciting bathroom. Elegant Georgian stone columns flank an enormous stone bath, once housed in an asylum, and lead scraps were cast in sea shells to make the tap heads, while the spout was made from an old copper downpipe. More copper piping was used to make the light above the cabinet, and the cabinet itself was constructed from old lead flashings. The slate shelf, skirtings and floor edging are all copings from a former school.

FAR RIGHT

A reclaimed terrazzo floor perfectly complements an informal dining-room.

In periods of austerity following two great wars, people adopted a 'make do and mend' mentality. Old clothes were cut up for dusters, scrap paper was turned into note pads and jam jars made handy containers. Household items and appliances were repaired rather than replaced. As the costs of running and maintaining large houses became prohibitive, many buildings of architectural merit were destroyed and with them much of our past was lost forever. Proud old timbers were burnt, mellow bricks were crushed for rubble and weathered roofing slates, imposing doors and ancient windows were discarded as useless.

As society grew more affluent, increasing quantities of waste were sent to landfill with potentially disastrous consequences.

Change has come slowly with the emergence of a more caring approach to our environment, fuelled by an appreciation of the detrimental effect we are having on the world's diminishing resources. We all help to create waste and that makes it a shared responsibility. The realisation of the need to conserve much of what had previously been rejected or destroyed has stimulated public interest in recycling. Global legislation and the introduction of government targets mean that the costs of managing and disposing of our waste will, in the future, become even greater.

Whether you are motivated by environmental concerns or just want to 'give it a go', the aim of this book is to show how salvage can be successfully incorporated into designs for both home and garden. It is amazing just what can be made from waste materials, cast-offs, 'rubbish'. Instead of throwing such things away without a second thought, we suggest ideas to resurrect them and perhaps make some unusual gifts. We are on a mission to demonstrate that it is possible to be both crafty and creative, taking one person's junk and fashioning it into another person's treasure! In *Recycle* we find interesting ways to give cast-offs a second life. We provide a structure within which you can be inventive, based on an awareness of what is available, keeping costs low and using tools you already own or ones that are easily obtainable. There are numerous inspirational photographs accompanying over 60 different projects grouped together in themed chapters:

This action-packed book is full of fun projects and practical ideas that are suitable for all levels of ability. Whether you are a keen beginner or an old hand, we urge you to *Recycle* – it's easier than you think!

RIGHT
Everything in the bathroom of this converted mid-nineteenth century church built by a pupil of Pugin has been salvaged. Curved panelling taken from the canopy above the organ has been cleverly used to disguise pipes, and the cistern has been hidden behind a pew and finished off with a slate shelf above.

An impressive floor-to-ceiling antique mirror forms the focal point of a grand dining room in Crispin and Elizabeth Deacon's home.

A large table automatically becomes the focal point in a dining area, because it is the place not only for eating and drinking but somewhere where family and friends spend time top is wooden, the beauty of the grain and the warmth of the wood can be seen to full advantage, contrasting with the surroundings of many of today's minimal, cool interiors. It may be

WINING AND DINING

together, gathering for discussions, celebrations and even business meetings. When sitting at a table you immediately see and have contact with a mass of surface, whether it is wood (the material traditionally used in the construction of tables) or zinc, stainless steel, stone or slate, all of which are good materials for rejuvenating an old table, depending on the surrounding decor. If the table a simple, functional design, with a scrubbed plank top, an oak, ash or elm surface supported on a trestle base, or something on a larger scale, altogether grander, perhaps made from hardwood with a highly polished surface and elegantly tapered legs. Whatever the style, a table may appear easy to design and make, but getting the design and proportions absolutely right can be quite a challenge.

NEAR RIGHT

Pine dressers rarely have such impact. The top half of this one, showing white china that is in use on a daily basis, was made up using reclaimed wood and then painted to match the old original base.

CENTRE LEFT

This circular kitchen table top was salvaged, repainted and screwed to a cast-iron base made from an agricultural root chopper (still bearing the maker's name) to make a highly individual and practical piece of furniture.

CENTRE RIGHT

Slate slabs from a Cornish farmhouse floor were made into tables and the wheels from a disused British Rail trolley used to make the feet bases; the decorative bracket was once a pub sign, and the window glass, coping stones and wooden floor are all reclaimed.

FAR RIGHT

An ornate gilded theatre box was located, refurbished and installed to great dramatic effect above the double folding doors leading from the dining room of the Charlton House Hotel.

LEFT

Despite its contemporary look, much of this kitchen by Milo Design has been reclaimed. Both the zinc sheets on the walls and the taps above the counter came from an old hospital, whilst the column and twin radiators were bought from a reclamation yard. The door handles just seen in the background are old trap door ring pulls, and the curvaceous kitchen counter came from a public house bar.

Wooden table tops need protection from very hot dishes, which can damage the surface. Practical, good-looking table mats are often difficult to find, but slate roofing tiles are easily available either directly from someone who may be reroofing or from the abundance of salvage yards to be found across the country. Cut down to size, varnished and backed with felt, they make stunning, indispensable place mats. (Mixing wedges of offcut tongue and groove timber in different colours, then joining them together, can make another unusual place mat.) To finish dressing the table, we have used ex-army aluminium dishes, which have been given an authentic pewter look and put to great effect as chargers, toning beautifully with the slate mats. Use clean empty baked bean tins filled with flowers and foliage and give new life to old bed springs as quirky candle holders (see page 122). Finally, to complete the look, recycle curtains, cushion covers, sheeting or any other suitable material from jumble sales and charity shops to make into napkins.

Traditionally dining chairs were made in oak, elm, ash, fruit-wood or a combination of two and sometimes three timbers, in hundreds of different designs, many of which are still reproduced today, though mostly in beech or pine.

Robust benches often make a convenient alternative to chairs when space is limited in an informal dining area, and they can be made quite easily using disused scaffold board. We show how a simple three-legged stool can be put together using a wooden chopping board for the seat and ash axe handles for the legs, just as salvaged tractor seats have also been made into comfortable kitchen stools.

With the warmth of the fire and the glow of the lights, wining and dining must surely be one of life's great pleasures.

SLATE TABLE MATS

EQUIPMENT

Tape measure
Straight edge
Marking point or sharp nail
Slate ripper
Pliers
Electric sander (optional)
Medium-grade glass- or emery paper
12 mm (½ in) paintbrush
Scissors
Glue brush

MATERIALS

Eight roof slates, overall size approx.
   40 x 30 cm (16 x 12 in)
Four larger roof slates, overall size approx.
   50 x 35 cm (20 x 14 in)
Satin finish or floor-grade varnish
Approx. 2 sq. m (2½ sq. yd) baize or felt
Rubberised glue

The materials above are sufficient to make a set of eight table mats and four centre mats. Adjust measurements as necessary according to the size of roof slates available. Also bear in mind the size of the table on which they will be placed.

METHOD

1 Select your slates carefully, rejecting any that are splitting, are too irregular in shape or have enlarged nail holes. Measure the slates from a good end and score a line across each width with the marking point or sharp nail. Use the slate ripper to cut slates to size, being careful to keep the cut edge as straight as possible. We suggest that the 40 x 30 cm (16 x 12 in) slates are cut down to 30 x 20 cm (12 x 8 in) and the 50 x 35 cm (20 x 14 in) slates are cut down to 35 x 25 cm (14 x 11 in).

2 All hand-split and cut slates have one face that is usually flat whilst the other has a chipped bevelled edge. The face with the bevelled edge will be the top of your place mat. Use pliers to trim the cut edge and the original edges to remove any loose material, matching the original bevelled edges if possible. Remove any loose material from both faces and finish with glass- or emery paper, either by hand or using a sander, taking care not to score the top surface too heavily. Wash each slate carefully in running water and leave to dry.

3 When both surfaces are dry, paint with two coats of satin finish or floor-grade varnish, covering any indentations and the bevelled edges. Leave to dry.

4 Cut twelve pieces of baize or felt 12 mm (½ in) smaller all round than the size of the slates. Brush rubberised glue on to the underside of the slates and fit the baize or felt on to the bottom surface; this will prevent your table mats scratching the table surface.

Safety note

We advise that you wear safety glasses or goggles when using any mechanical sanding equipment. Rubber or protective gloves are also recommended for this project.

Food is one of our growing passions – if the number of cookery books and television programmes is anything to go by – and the social importance of family meals is widely recognised, yet how much thought do we give to the presentation of the daily eating ritual? Making the table look as exciting as the dishes themselves takes just a little thought and effort, and here we suggest one idea to rejuvenate roof slates to make easy but chic replacements for melamine mats bearing images of Big Ben and the leaning tower of Pisa. These slate mats will give your table a new, crisp image, and by scouring skips parked outside properties in the process of being reroofed, demolished or restored, you are sure to find enough slates to make up a table setting for ten or more.

If raiding skips is not your style, another source of old roofing slate is your nearest reclamation yard. The slate will have suffered from exposure to wind, rain, snow and pollution, but it is still desirable. Newly cut slate can be purchased from any flooring contractor, tile shop or builders' merchant, where you will be faced with a mind-boggling choice of colour, size and thickness.

Damaged or chipped roofing slates can be cut down to the required size and the underside covered in felt or baize to protect the table surface. Once cleaned and polished, the slate's inherent insulating qualities, combined with its practical wipe-clean surface, make it a smart table accessory to be admired (and no doubt copied) when you next decide to hold a dinner party.

INFORMAL DINING

There is a proliferation of companies providing conservatories whose selling pitch has long been to persuade us to take the 'inside out', but the owners of this country kitchen decided to bring the 'outside in' when it came to decorating an informal family eating area.

Inspired by the potting shed and a collection of old tools – most of which were handmade, although some of their origins were rather obscure – their interpretation of the look began to take shape with the tool display, not the table, being the main focal point. Although the building was fairly old, its interior had been insensitively modernised at some stage in its history, leaving little of its original charm. With a blank canvas and a limited budget, they set to work.

Natural light was poor, so the walls were painted off-white and an old ledge-and-brace exterior door, complete with its original chipped and flaking paint, was installed. In order to make the 'shed' more intimate, they disguised the ceiling with suspended rows of redundant wooden ladders; this gave the room a warmer, more welcoming feel and provided somewhere to hang baskets, herbs and other decorative items. The ladders were obtained very inexpensively from a quaintly old-fashioned horticultural nursery that had ceased trading after the death of the elderly owner, for they were regarded as unsafe once they were superseded by modern metal versions.

The classic refectory table was made from disused scaffold boards and the chapel chairs have an ecclesiastical past, as the name suggests. A stool and a chopping block were made using axe handles in ash for the legs; soft, atmospheric lighting in the form of a floor-standing candle lamp was created from a one-time flower display stand, and a stencil candle light made an interesting table centrepiece. To complete the look, assorted garden sieves and an ancient saw were used as attractive wall displays and faux pewter plates adorned the window sill.

TOOL DISPLAY

EQUIPMENT

25 mm (1 in) paintbrush
Waxing brush or stiff-bristled paintbrush
Soft cotton rag
Fine-grade wire wool
Proprietary metal polish
Wire brush
Electric drill
Circular wire brush or sanding flap
    drill head
3 mm (⅛ in) wood drill bit
Screwdriver
Pliers

MATERIALS

Selection of old tools
Wooden braced plank display board
Colourless timber preservative
Antique brown furniture wax
Clear wax or metal lacquer spray
Selection of screws and rawlplugs
Medium metal wire or gardening wire
Length of batten approx. 25 mm (1 in) x
    75 mm (3 in) x the width of the display
    board

Safety note

We advise that you wear safety glasses or goggles
when using any mechanical sanding equipment.
Rubber or other protective gloves are
recommended for this project.

Old farm equipment, kitchen utensils and garden tools are still easy to find, inexpensive to buy and have a character sadly missing in much of the equipment produced today.

Enthusiastic readers of the local press will find farm and market garden sales advertised. As small growers and farmers retire, their families may be reluctant to continue to work on what are often uncommercial holdings and the land is sold to surrounding farmers or purchased by urban dwellers seeking a rural retreat. A result of this change is the disposal of what were often the everyday tools used by past generations. Many of the tools were made by local foundries or fabricated by the landowner using skills now forgotten and the purpose of some of them is quite obscure. Walls displaying old shovels, pitchforks, rakes of odd shapes and sizes, some complete, a few broken and many of a particularly local design, are a constant source of intrigue.

For this project we have used a selection of farm and garden tools displayed on an old wooden surface. The tools include a redundant spring grain weight with a brass face which was only revealed after the offending dirt was laboriously removed, a hand-forged drainage spade, a pruning saw, a short flat-tined fork, the origin of which remains unknown, a brass and iron stirrup pump, a primitive sickle and a pair of fencing pliers. These tools were only a small part of a selection of begrimed and broken tools bought as one lot at a farm auction for less than half the price of a modern hand trowel.

TOOL DISPLAY

METHOD

1 Treat the display board with colourless timber preservative and leave to dry. Then apply antique brown furniture wax with the waxing brush or stiff-bristled paintbrush, rubbing it well into the wood with a soft cotton rag and polish to a soft sheen with more soft cotton rag. A second coat of wax can be applied, which will give a deeper colour and longer-lasting finish. Put to one side.

2 To clean brass or copper surfaces, use a proprietary metal polish and fine-grade wire wool, finishing with more polish applied with a soft cloth. Seal polished surfaces with metal lacquer to prevent subsequent tarnishing. Wooden handles and parts should be washed in warm soapy water then waxed and polished with furniture wax. Clean iron or steel tools with a wire brush to remove loose rust and dirt, then finish with an electric drill fitted with a circular wire brush or sanding flap drill head.

3 Use the drill and wire or sanding flap head to remove corrosion until the desired finish is achieved. The metal surface of the tool will be pitted more or less deeply depending on the amount of corrosion it has suffered; the aim of this cleaning is not to return the tool to its original condition but to remove surface rust and reveal the colour of the base metal. To preserve the finish and prevent subsequent corrosion, either apply clear wax to the surface or spray with metal lacquer.

4 Place the board on two blocks above a flat surface, so that you can work on both sides, and experiment with arranging the cleaned tools on the front until you have a display that pleases you. Wooden-handled tools can be fixed to the board using screws driven in from the reverse. Remove each tool, carefully noting its position, and use the electric drill and 3 mm (⅛ in) drill bit to drill a hole from the top where the handle will be placed. Replace the tool and, working from the back of the board, drive a screw through the board and into the handle, securing the tool to the board.

5 Metal tools can be fitted to the board using medium wire or garden wire. Use a malleable coated wire of a muted colour or one with a dull finish, otherwise the wire will be obvious and spoil the appearance of the finished display. Select a part of the tool that will support it when the board is returned to the vertical and drill holes close to each side of the tool. Cut a length of wire, bend it into a 'U' shape, then pass it over the tool and through both holes so that each end emerges by at least 50 mm (2 in) on the reverse. Use pliers to twist the ends of wire together to secure the tool to the board.

When all the tools are fitted, remove the board from the blocks and place it upright to ensure that all the tools are securely in place. Tighten any screws or wire, as necessary, or add more fixings if required. Take the length of batten and fix it to the wall in the desired position with screws and rawlplugs. Place the board on the wall, resting a brace on the fixed batten. Once you are satisfied with its position, secure it with two screws through the board into the batten.

FLOWER DISPLAY CANDLE STAND

EQUIPMENT

Wire brush
Small stiff brush (an old toothbrush
   is ideal)
12 mm (½ in) paintbrush
Soft brush or cotton rag

MATERIALS

Flower stand
Stove blacking paste
Selection of small metal tart and
   confectionery cups
Matt black paint or spray paint
White spirit
Night lights or tea lights
Candle
Scented oils

Safety note

Rubber or protective gloves are
recommended for this project.

Auctions are a good hunting ground for interesting items. We bought several 'bargains' at the auction of the contents of a nursery and garden centre, including a number of cast-iron stands once used to display bunches of fresh cut flowers.

The stands had not been used for many years and the original paintwork had almost completely rusted away. Constructed of a hollow iron column set in a heavy cast hexagonal base, each stand came with a number of bent metal display platforms designed to fit over the column and fix at any height with a turn screw. Perhaps not surprisingly, there was little demand at the auction for such idiosyncratic items and we were able to buy them for next to nothing. It is unlikely that similar stands are easy to find, but the new use we found for them illustrates how, by using a little imagination, the most unwanted items can be salvaged and resuscitated. Place plain or fluted individual metal confectionery tins from government surplus stores (individual aluminium apple tart bases will do just as well) into the metal platforms and fill some with night lights and others with aromatic essential oils – an idea to please the eye and soothe the senses. Alternatively, remove the platforms, keeping just the heavy bases and pole and have an electrician wire the stand (unless you are confident enough to undertake this yourself) and convert it into a low standard lamp. Painted and fitted with a simple shade, it takes on a cool contemporary look, far removed from its original purpose.

FLOWER DISPLAY CANDLE STAND

METHOD

1 We chose to convert this stand into a candelabra and give it a muted satin black finish. Had the stand been completely rusted rather than patchy with some of the original paint still adhering to it, we would have wire brushed it and sealed the finish with a metal lacquer to preserve its rusted appearance. Remove the metal platforms (each comprising two sets of four branches welded to a central pipe) from the column, and ensure the turn screws work freely; apply releasing oil if necessary. Use the wire brush to remove loose rust and peeling paint from the base, column and platforms, making sure to wire brush any residual paint to provide a key for the stove blacking finish.

2 Place the stand and platforms on newspaper or other protective surface and, with the small stiff brush, apply the stove blacking to all exposed parts, paying particular attention to the corroded metal to ensure total coverage of all surfaces. Leave to dry to a matt black finish. When the blacking is completely dry, polish the stand and platforms to a soft sheen with a soft brush or rag. Continue until little or no polish is deposited on the rag and the blacking does not come off when the stand is handled. Replace the platforms on the stand in the positions desired, and secure with the turn screws.

3 For candle holders we used a selection of round and fluted metal tart and confectionery cups, old and rusty and long past their useful life, which we found in a government surplus store and which fitted the platform rings perfectly. (Only later did we discover that aluminium tart cups used by most manufacturing bakeries would have been just as suitable.) Brush or spray paint the cups matt black, both inside and out, and leave to dry. Place a night light or tea light into each cup and fit the cups into the rings. We fitted night lights into the larger cups and filled the smaller fluted cups with scented oils. Finally, fit a candle into the top of the stand column and light the night lights; as the oils in the fluted cups warm, their perfume will permeate the room.

STENCIL LIGHT

EQUIPMENT

Scissors or craft knife

MATERIALS

Eighteen equally sized stencils, either
    letters or numbers
Adhesive metal tape
Candle and candle holder

METHOD

1 Select half the stencils and place them front side down on a flat surface. Carefully arrange them together to make a rectangle three stencils wide by three stencils deep. Most old stencils were hand cut and so sizes are slightly irregular; when fitting them together make sure that the edges of your rectangle are square.

2 Use the scissors or craft knife to cut lengths of adhesive metal tape to the height and width of the rectangle. Carefully remove the backing and lay the tape along the joints between the stencils to join them together, using a finger to rub down the tape to ensure good adhesion. Repeat with the remaining nine stencils to make a second, similarly sized rectangle.

3 Cut two lengths of tape to the height of the rectangles. Remove the backing from one and join the two rectangles to make one piece six stencils wide by three deep. Carefully bring the two ends of the rectangle together to make a cylinder; place your hand inside and join the ends together with the remaining cut length of tape. Again, rub down all newly taped joints with your finger to ensure adequate adhesion.

Stand the candle holder and candle on a flat surface and place the newly constructed stencil light over them. The metal tape should be sufficiently malleable to allow the stencils to be manipulated into a regular hexagonal shape. Light the candle and enjoy the muted illumination cast from this simple, yet charming, candle light.

Stencils have been in use for many years to mark cartons, boxes, crates, bales and all sorts of shipped and carried goods. Made from a variety of materials including zinc, steel, tin, cardboard and even brass, stencils are still in use today, even in this age of technology, although most modern designs are manufactured from moulded plastic and lack the allure of their earlier counterparts. We have managed to amass several full sets of stencils over the years; most are made of zinc but one particularly valued set is made from copper sheet. For this project we have used a set of more commonly available zinc stencils that came from a farm sale and were bought in their original box complete with brushes and inks. The stencils had been heavily used and were stained with ink, but we chose to use them in this condition rather than attempt to clean them.

The particular joy of stencils when used for a lighting project such as this is that the lettering cut-outs cast curious illuminations and make a charming display of light and shade. This project demonstrates the making of a very basic candle light, but the more ambitious craftsperson might attempt the construction of a light column, shade or wall light.

PEWTER PLATES

EQUIPMENT

Metal cleaning paste
Medium-grade wire wool
Soft cotton rag

MATERIALS

Aluminium plates or bowls
Metal polish
Antique brown furniture wax
Metal lacquer spray

METHOD

1 Carefully select the plates you will be using for this project. All will show the effects of years of wear and tear and will be scored with cutlery marks very similar to the surface markings seen on most antique pewter, but this is part of its charm. Many plates are stamped with a government or maker's mark on their top surface; these should be rejected. Instead choose plates that are unmarked and are not too damaged or dented.

2 Place a small amount of metal cleaner (we used a proprietary stainless steel cleaner) on an old plate or other container, dip a wad of wire wool in the cleaner and begin to work on the surface of the plate. Always rub round the surface and keep the wad of wire wool saturated with cleaner. Continue working until any surface oxidation is removed and the wire wool is working into the surface of the aluminium. Periodically wipe the surface clean with the soft cotton rag to examine the finish. Be careful not to rub out all the surface scratches and markings.

3 When you are satisfied with the appearance you have achieved, wipe the plate clean and apply polish with the soft cloth, rubbing it well into the surface. Wipe the surface clean and

polish with more clean soft cloth. Now you must examine the plate and decide on its final colour and finish. The cleaner and polish will have darkened the appearance of the plate, but an even darker finish can be achieved by rubbing a little antique brown furniture wax into the surface. Apply the wax liberally and wipe off, leaving a residue on the surface before allowing it to dry and polishing it. You may wish to stop at this point because the wax will prevent further tarnishing.

4 Should you wish to achieve a gloss finish, spray the plate with metal lacquer and leave it to dry. Your faux pewter plates will deceive all but the most knowledgeable observer, unless they pick them up in which case their lightness will reveal the fraud. Display the plates on a dresser or shelf, use plate stretchers to hang them on a wall or use them as chargers under plates at the dining table. Lacquered plates may be washed in hot water, and waxed plates should be dusted clean, but remember that they should not be used for eating purposes.

Safety note

We advise that rubber or protective gloves are used for this project and that you work on newspaper or some other disposable surface.

ewter is an alloy of tin and lead, ometimes with the addition of a ttle copper or antimony, which in ast years was used for plates, nugs and other vessels as a ubstitute for the wooden or orous earthenware vessels used reviously. Lead is highly toxic, so would be unwise to use early ewter for food or drink. Because f the awareness of this danger, nodern pewter uses considerably ss lead in its manufacture.

Early pewter is very collectable nd fetches high prices at uctions or in antique shops. Vhen polished, it assumes a dull, ttractive sheen, and a collection f old pewter arranged on a resser or mantle makes a nemorable display.

Quite recently we discovered a umber of discarded aluminium lates and bowls that we thought night lend themselves to onversion into faux pewter, and his project demonstrates our nethod. We later learnt that these lates were examples of nousands that were once roduced for the army during and st after the 1940s and which ccasionally turn up in overnment surplus stores all over ne country.

AXE-HANDLE STOOL

EQUIPMENT

Tape measure
Electric drill
25 mm (1 in) spade wood bit
12 mm (½ in) straight or rounded wood
    chisel
Hammer or mallet
Variable-speed multi-purpose electric tool
    with 18 mm (¾ in) sanding head (or
    round wood file)
Soft cotton rag
Medium-grade glass paper

MATERIALS

Timber round approx. 35 cm (14 in)
    diameter x 38 mm (1½ in) deep
Three axe handles or three 60 cm (24 in)
    lengths of broom handle
Scrap timber
Wood glue

Many of the 'bargains' found in a
reclamation yard or scavenged
from a skip or rubbish tip remain
in our workshop to this day, half
forgotten, awaiting the visionary
ideas for which they were originall
so enthusiastically acquired.

One such purchase was a
stack of dirt-encrusted axe
handles found at a government
surplus yard buried under a pile c
discarded ammunition boxes and
offered for sale as firewood. Their
interesting shapes caught our eye
and on closer inspection we
realised they were made of solid
ash. Determined they would not
end up as fuel for the fire, we
managed to secure some and nov
we wish we had bought more.

The shape of the axe handles
seemed to suggest legs and so
we used three for the legs of a
kitchen chopping block. In this
project we show how they can be
used to construct a charming if
unconventional stool. A discarded
beech round, probably originally
made as a chopping board, was
used to make the seat. The axe
handles will also make the sides
of a log basket, and, should you
manage to buy a quantity, they
would make an eye-catching
balustrade. If you have difficulty in
finding axe handles, the stool can
be made just as easily from
broom handles, offcut timber or
even straight branches pruned
from a tree.

When making this stool, the
legs should be slightly splayed fo
stability, and all the holes for
housing the legs should be cut at
a slight angle to allow for this
splay. For the seat of the stool, a
similar round can be cut from a
solid or laminated timber offcut.

AXE-HANDLE STOOL

METHOD

1 Mark three points on the top surface at an equal distance round the circumference of the timber round and approximately 25 mm (1 in) from the edge. Place the handles or other material being used for the legs inside these marked points and draw round them with a pencil to mark where the legs will be inserted.

2 Place the round on a piece of scrap timber and use the spade bit, driven in at a slight angle, to make an initial hole. To prevent the timber splitting, drill through from one face of the timber until the point of the spade bit just emerges and then complete the hole drilling from the opposite side. Repeat, drilling holes for all three legs. If you are using broom handles for the legs, use a spade bit the size of the handles.

3 Use the variable-speed multi-purpose electric sander or chisel and wood file to enlarge the hole to the size of the pencil mark, making sure that the angle of splay is maintained. If you are making the legs from broom handle, there should be no necessity to enlarge the spade-drilled holes.

4 Apply wood glue liberally to the first 25 mm (1 in) of one of the axe handles and insert it into the round from the underside. Tap it gently home with a hammer or mallet until the top is flush with, or proud of, the upper surface of the round. Axe handles are made with a slit cut in their top to allow a wedge to be inserted when fitted to the axe head. Cut a small wedge from offcut timber to the width of this slit, apply glue and drive it into the top of the handle to secure it firmly into the round. If you are using broom handle, cut a 38 mm (1½ in) slit in its top to allow wedging into the round for added security and strength.

Wipe off any excess glue and leave the stool on one side for the glue to dry. Sand off any excess glue or timber proud of the top surface and finish as desired. The completed stool can be waxed, stained or painted. If you choose staining, ensure that any glue on the wood surface is removed before you apply the stain, because the dried glue will not absorb the stain and so the finish will be patchy. The stool top we made for this project was completed with a distressed paint finish and the legs were waxed with antique brown furniture wax.

An oak bed by furniture designer John Edmonds made from three-hundred-year-old beams taken from the roof of an ancient barn which had collapsed as a result of neglect. The headboard insert is natural woven willow.

Whether the style is comfortably traditional or has a Zen-like simplicity, bedrooms are where we spend a third of our lives. Careful thought and

The amount of light largely depends on the direction in which the bedroom faces, and light, whether daylight or interior lighting, will to some extent dictate its mood and colours.

BEDROOMS, BATHROOMS AND BOUDOIRS

consideration need to be given to how we treat our bedrooms, which are certainly the most personal rooms in the house, if not the most important. Besides the bed, a bedroom may have space for additional furniture, perhaps an armchair, sofa or table, as well as storage items such as chests of drawers and wardrobes, making them not just rooms to sleep in but also a place to read and relax.

Furnishing fabrics are fun to think about: bedcovers, cushions, loose covers and throws for the chairs. Linen has for years been a firm favourite, especially old French country linen sheets of superb quality, roughly textured, often with a red embroidered monogram at one end and occasionally a fringe. They make simple but effective beautifully draping curtains, allowing light to filter through.

TOP

This bed with dancing figures by Paul Anderson is constructed of old oak joists and the remains of defunct oak gates. It demonstrates the designer's love of using old wood with a visible history, showing all the colour variations which develop naturally in oak over time.

BOTTOM

With a strong dislike for conventional free-standing wardrobes, the owner bought a pair of handsome hardwood double doors – probably of Indian origin – and used them to conceal a walk-in wardrobe.

Children have their own ideas when it comes to decorating their bedrooms, and it is strong, bright colours that usually appeal to them. They like their own special piece of furniture, such as an old school desk that has been rescued and transformed from a grubby object emblazoned with graffiti into something revitalised, practical and fun. Older children and teenagers want to use their bedrooms as somewhere to escape from the grown-ups; here, surrounded by chaotic mess, they can play loud music, hence the need for CD storage. We show you how to make practical CD storage out of a dilapidated old wooden French shutter (see pages 54–57).

The bed is an obvious feature or focal point in the bedroom. Beds are made from many different materials, most commonly wood, but also iron and brass, and a bed made from an unusual material such as aluminium will give a very contemporary feel to a bedroom. Beds come in all shapes and sizes and although there are specialist companies who will make up unusual mattress dimensions, including round or even boat-shaped ones, it is useful to bear in mind if constructing a bed to your own design from salvaged materials that mattresses are easier and cheaper to obtain in standard sizes. Whatever its size and shape, it is important to always buy the best-quality mattress you can afford.

Finding timber suitable for constructing beds is often easier than you might think. Old railway sleepers and ceiling beams of oak and elm can all be cut to size and used to make the framework, just as redundant carved doors, church pews, decorative wooden panels and even disused five-bar farm gates are the perfect raw materials for making into practical and interesting beds or headboards. A highly unusual fold-away guest bed is shown opposite, imaginatively made from an

exquisitely painted panel depicting animals from Noah's Ark which was salvaged from a fairground ride.

The idea that bathrooms should be spartan, purely functional, hygienic rooms containing a cast-iron bath, pedestal wash basin, lavatory and lino-covered floor is fortunately long gone.

Bathrooms today are expected to be every bit as comfortable as any other room in the house. Just take the briefest look through any of the glossy magazines and you will see rooms purporting to be bathrooms but looking more like stage sets – all opulence and atmosphere – or cosy and homely, the epitome of rustic country charm. Idiosyncratic items add interest and character, such as a single trestle bracketed to the wall and used as a rail to show off pretty towels and linens (see pages 42–43). Enormous cupboards in rich mahogany or other hardwoods, too big and cumbersome for the average-sized room today, can be cut down in size to panel a bath, perhaps continuing around the walls to dado height, and can even made into cupboard doors under the basins to provide additional storage.

Because we lead increasingly busy lives with more and more pressures, there seems to be a need to simplify things, to have order, comfort and harmony in our homes. One way of achieving this is to optimise space and create storage – a place for everything and everything in its place. Old hardwood 'first class' railway compartments can be salvaged and made into capacious cupboards for the dressing room or boudoir. Enormous, superbly carved mahogany wardrobes, which would cost the earth if the equivalent quality were made today, look just as handsome and majestic when made to fit an alcove or any other space.

TOP LEFT

This unusual spare bed, which folds up against the wall when not in use, is an original 1933 fairground Noah's Ark design, comprising two horses and chariots. On the bed is a salvaged traditional southern Italian family-sized bedcover, and in the background is a mural painted by Corrina Sargood to disguise a wall-to-wall cupboard containing an office desk and storage.

TOP RIGHT

Black and white are used with striking effect in Elizabeth and Crispin Deacon's guest bathroom, its 1930s sanitary fittings juxtaposed with contemporary lighting.

RIGHT

A view of the bathroom of Hank and Sophia Terry, the owners of Milo Design. The shower walls and mirror frame are made from old lead roofing sheet and the soap dish/shampoo rack has been created from a lightning conductor salvaged from a church. The wash basin was cleverly fashioned from the base of an old copper hot water tank and the tap heads were cast from lead roof flashing in a child's jelly mould.

RAILWAY BED

EQUIPMENT

Tape measure
Set square
Hammer
32 mm (1¼ in) wood chisel
Handsaw
Glasspaper
Electric drill and bits
Screwdriver
Adjustable spanner
38 mm (1½ in) paintbrush
Soft cotton rag

MATERIALS

Four posts
Approx. 2 m (6 ft 6 in) of 22.5 cm x 25 mm
   (9 x 1 in) planed timber
Wood glue
65 mm (2½ in) wood screws
90 cm (3 ft) single metal bed frame and
   headboard fittings (chills)
Wood stain
Clear furniture wax

Amidst the pile of debris our eyes were drawn to the tapering wooden poles protruding above the rusty metal ammunition boxes, military bed bases stacked one upon the other, enough rainwater-filled latrines to equip an entire barracks and assorted shovels.

Filthy, wet and shivering, we stood in the biting wind on a November morning speculating on what the poles had been used for and how they could be used again. Inspiration struck: their slender shapes lent themselves perfectly to a design for a bed, a four-poster bed to be precise. We quickly acquired a job lot. We later learnt from Lawrence, owner of Harper's Bazaar and purveyor of all things surplus to government needs, that they were solid ash levers used on the railways to move wagons around the sidings by hand before mechanisation made them obsolete. If you cannot obtain ash levers such as these, the bed could just as easily be constructed using any pillar-like objects, such as fence posts or staircase newel posts.

The metal bed frame and head-board fittings were located in a salvage yard. Almost forty years old, they had once been turned out in their thousands. They were robustly constructed for use in army barracks but had never been used and apart from some surface rust, were in perfect condition. If you can't find a similar frame, you can buy one new from a small number of specialist contract furniture makers. This bed could also be made with a slatted timber base set into wooden side pieces fitted to the headboard using any of the numerous connectors on the market.

RAILWAY BED

METHOD

Before commencing work on this project, read through the instructions and think carefully about how you will approach the making of your bed and its dimensions. Remember that you will need to find or purchase a mattress for the bed and that most are made to standard sizes. As a guide, single beds are normally constructed so that the mattress top is approximately 45–50 cm (18–20 in) from floor level and you will have to adapt the project for the mattress you propose to use. Should you wish to provide storage under the bed, it can be made higher, although it is a good idea to keep to a height such that you can sit comfortably on the edge of the bed.

1 Make a mark with a pencil at the proposed height of the bed frame on the inside face of one of the posts. Place the headboard fitting (chill) on the post so that the bed frame, when attached, will be fixed at that height. Mark the screw holes and make two marks, one above and one below the screw holes, 10 cm (4 in) apart, centred on the screw holes. Use the set square to transfer these measurements across the inside and down two sides of the post. Measure the exact thickness of the 22.5 cm (9 in) timber plank and draw a line that measurement deep on the two sides across the 10 cm (4 in) pencil lines. Use the hammer and wood chisel to score a line along this mark which shows the areas to be cut out of the post to house the 22.5 cm (9 in) head and foot boards. Turn the post inside face up and with a handsaw make a series of cuts approximately 12 mm (½ in) apart and 25 mm (1 in) deep, using the chiselled line as a guide for the exact depth, for the full length of the 10 cm (4 in) marked area.

2 When you have made saw cuts across the whole width of the post, insert the wood chisel into the cuts and gently lever out the waste wood. Clean the cut rebate with the wood chisel and glasspaper, making sure to keep to the depth indicated by the scored lines. Now repeat this process using another post; these two will hold the headboard.

3 Measure the exact width of your bed frame from fixing bolt (or bolt hole) to fixing bolt. Measure the width of a post and add it to this measurement. Use the set square to mark that final measurement on the planed timber plank and cut it to size. Lay the cut plank on a work surface and use the set square and pencil to mark a line the width of the post across each end. Mark two lines 10 cm (4 in) apart at each end centred on the width of the plank, and extend them to join the lines marking the width of the post. Use the handsaw to cut away the two outer sections at each end, each of which will measure approximately 65 mm (2½ in) x the width of the post, to create a simple T joint at each end. Err on the side of caution when cutting: it is better to cut these pieces out too small, and to have to sand down the joints to fit the rebates cut in the posts, than to remove too much timber and be left with loose joints.

4 Put plenty of wood glue into the rebate cut in the first post, then insert one of the cut joints. Check with the set square that the joint is true, then drill and fix with 65 mm (2½ in) wood screws. It is advisable before finally joining to replace the headboard fitting (chill) and check that its screw holes do not correspond with the screws holding the joint. Repeat this process, inserting the other joint into the second post, and you have created the headboard for your bed.

Wipe off any excess wood glue and put the assembled pieces to one side for the glue to dry completely. Now follow the same directions to construct the footboard with the second two posts and remaining length of timber plank.

5 Replace the headboard fittings (chills) on the foot- and headboards and secure with screws driven through the joints into the wood of the posts.

6 You will probably need assistance with this part of the project. Lean the headboard up against a vertical surface and balance one end of the bed frame on its headboard fittings (chills). Raise the other end of the frame and manoeuvre the footboard so that the bed frame can be dropped into place over its fittings. Half tighten the integral nuts fitted into the bed frame to secure it first to the footboard then to the headboard. Use a spanner to tighten all the nuts to make a rigid frame.

When we had assembled the bed we decided that because the colours of the ash wood bed posts and the salvaged pitch pine end boards were so different, we would stain the whole bed a mid-oak colour to give some uniformity to its appearance. This had the additional advantage of masking the lighter tones of the exposed timber where ends had been sawn. After applying the stain with a cotton rag, we finished the bed with a light coat of clear furniture wax and polished it with more soft cotton rag. Installed in a spare room and fitted with a mattress, the bed was made up with a cotton-covered duvet and down-filled pillow and made welcoming with a natural sheepskin thrown over its foot.

TRESTLE TOWEL RAIL

EQUIPMENT

Tape measure
Handsaw
Paint scraper
Electric sander
Glasspaper
42 mm (1¾ in) paintbrush
Lint-free cotton rag
Electric hammer drill
Masonry drill bit
Wood drill bit to fit 65 mm (2½ in) screws
Screwdriver

MATERIALS

Wooden trestle
White translucent wood finish or white matt
    emulsion paint and satin finish acrylic
    varnish
Length 65 x 38 mm (2½ x 1½ in) planed
    softwood timber
65 mm (2½ in) rawlpugs
65 mm (2½ in) screws
Four 38 mm (1½ in) angle (or corner)
    brackets
18 mm (¾ in) screws

Safety note

We advise that you wear
safety glasses or goggles when
using any mechanical sanding
equipment; a dust mask is also
sensible in case the surface to
be sanded has been previously
finished with a lead-based paint.
Rubber or protective gloves
are also recommended for
this project.

METHOD

1 Measure the site where the towel rail will be
installed, then measure the trestle. If it is too
long to fit in the selected site, allowing for at least
a 15 cm (6 in) gap below the trestle and a similar
or greater gap above, trim it to size with the
handsaw. Remove flaked or loose paint with the
paint scraper and sand to a smooth finish with
the electric sander and glasspaper. It is not
necessary to remove all residual paint, just to
produce a smooth base for the wood finish. Use
the electric sander to smooth off all newly sawn
sharp edges and corners.

2 Apply a liberal coat of white translucent
wood finish or matt white emulsion paint.
Leave for several minutes until part dried, then
wipe over the surface with the clean cotton rag
to remove some of the surface colour, leaving a
residual finish on the timber surface. Use your
judgement to create the finish you want – the
process can be repeated until the desired result
is achieved. Leave the trestle to dry. If you have
used matt emulsion paint, seal with two coats of
satin finish acrylic varnish.

3 Measure the width of the trestle at the top
and bottom rungs, then use the handsaw to
cut two lengths of the 65 x 38 mm (2½ x 1½ in)
planed softwood timber to these measurements
to make wall battens. Ideally, these should be
painted in the same colour as the wall on which
the trestle towel rail is to be fitted; if not, they
should be finished to match the trestle. Add 15
cm (6 in) to the height of the trestle and use the
drill and masonry drill bit to attach the top batten
to the wall at this point with rawlplugs and 65
mm (2½ in) screws. Offer up the trestle and mark
the position of the bottom rung on the wall, then
attach the bottom batten in the same way. This
will raise the trestle base approximately 15 cm
(6 in) off the floor. Fit the 38 mm (1½ in) angle (or
corner) brackets to the rear of the trestle behind
the top and bottom rungs with the 18 mm (¾ in)
screws, positioning them so that when the trestle
is mounted on the battens the brackets will be
concealed behind the rungs. Secure the trestle to
the battens with more 18 mm (¾ in) screws.

Flicking through the pages of the glossy magazines over recent years you will have seen a number of bamboo or wooden ladders used as props in interior photographs because they lend themselves to obvious display stands. Ours is not a ladder but a trestle, often used in the painting and decorating trade as the portable base for a plank top. It had been painted at some stage and, rather than sand the paint off, we chose to keep its worn and aged patina and seal it with a satin varnish because it toned so well with other pieces of furniture with a similar 'driftwood' effect. Trestles can be found in various sizes, and should you wish to secure yours on brackets to the wall for use as a clothes rack, towel rail or any other practical use you may think of, you will first need to consider the height of the ceiling and the proportions of the room.

A PRE-TEEN BEDROOM

Children usually have a very good idea of how they like their bedrooms to look, especially when they approach their teenage years. This bedroom is not typical – it's tidy for a start! However, it does house some noteworthy reclaimed artefacts, such as the sturdy old school desk, painted with a distress finish, a wall-hung roof slate blackboard for jotting down homework deadlines, wire letter baskets to hold exercise books and, in pride of place, a painted wooden window shutter fixed to the wall and used to store the young occupant's CD collection. Another clever storage idea is the pair of wooden ladders (originally one long one, cut in half) with zinc shelving from a government surplus store slotted over the rungs. The shelving was originally used as racking for storing tinned food in a civil defence underground shelter, built in case of a nuclear attack, but with the end of the Cold War the shelter was closed down and the contents disposed of. Extra shelves can be added as the book collection expands.

SCHOOL DESK

EQUIPMENT

Screwdriver
Sash clamps
Electric sander
Medium-grade glasspaper
38 mm (1½ in) paintbrush
Waxing brush or stiff-bristled paintbrush
Soft cotton rag

MATERIALS

Traditional wooden school desk
Wood glue
Wood filler
Dark blue (or selected colour) matt
    emulsion paint
Antique brown furniture wax
Matt black emulsion paint

Safety note

We advise that you wear safety glasses or goggles
when using any mechanical sanding equipment.
Rubber or protective gloves are also
recommended for this project.

The design for a traditional child's desk, made of beech and oak and produced in their thousands for schools up and down the country, has never been surpassed for rugged practicality. These desks are, however, slowly being replaced, as budgets allow, by tables or desks often manufactured in plywood or laminate.

These days, hard-pressed schools are constrained to keep to tight financial budgets, and many caretakers spend much of their time repairing old, graffiti-covered desks and cannibalising others to keep them in use for as long as possible. You may be fortunate to find a school that has just received a new consignment of furniture; if so, there is every chance that, in return for a small donation to school funds, they will be pleased to release from the store a battered but not irreparable sample.

A salvaged solid timber school desk is well worth the time and effort required to repair and refurbish it, because it is ideally suited to a child's bedroom, providing useful storage and an essential surface on which to write, even in this technology-driven age. We have chosen to give the desk a distressed paint finish to soften its appearance.

SCHOOL DESK

METHOD

1 The extent of the damage to the desk will dictate how much repair should be undertaken, but, whatever its apparent condition, we suggest that all metalwork should be removed and the desk taken apart.

2 Inspect all joints for damage and repair as necessary. Carefully apply wood glue to all joints and reassemble using sash clamps to secure the joints. Use the electric sander and medium-grade glasspaper to remove all the varnish and most of the inevitable graffiti, carved initials and other evidence of children's use. Fill any large holes or scratches with wood filler.

3 Paint the exterior of the desk with one coat of dark blue (or selected colour) matt emulsion. Leave to dry for at least twenty-four hours.

4 When the paint is fully dry, use glasspaper to remove paint carefully from edges, where wear would naturally occur. For authenticity, pay particular attention to corners, stretchers (if your desk has any) and legs, where feet would normally cause wear.

5 Use the waxing brush or stiff-bristled paintbrush to apply a liberal application of antique brown furniture wax to a small area, then rub it into the paint with a soft cotton rag. It is best to work with a well-waxed rag to prevent dragging. The wax will react with the surface of the paint to give a distressed appearance; the previously sanded areas will pick up some colour from the paint, but this will serve to give a look of natural wear. Leave to dry and continue working on other areas until the desk is finished. When all the wax is dry, polish with the stiff brush and finish with a clean soft cotton rag.

Paint the inside of the desk with matt black emulsion paint. It will prove almost impossible to remove all the ink stains and other marks on the inside surface, so painting it black or another dark colour is the best course of action.

Reassemble the desk, replacing all the metal parts using the original or similar cross-head screws. The finished desk may be cleaned with a moistened soft cloth and will benefit from an occasional application of clear furniture wax to maintain its appearance.

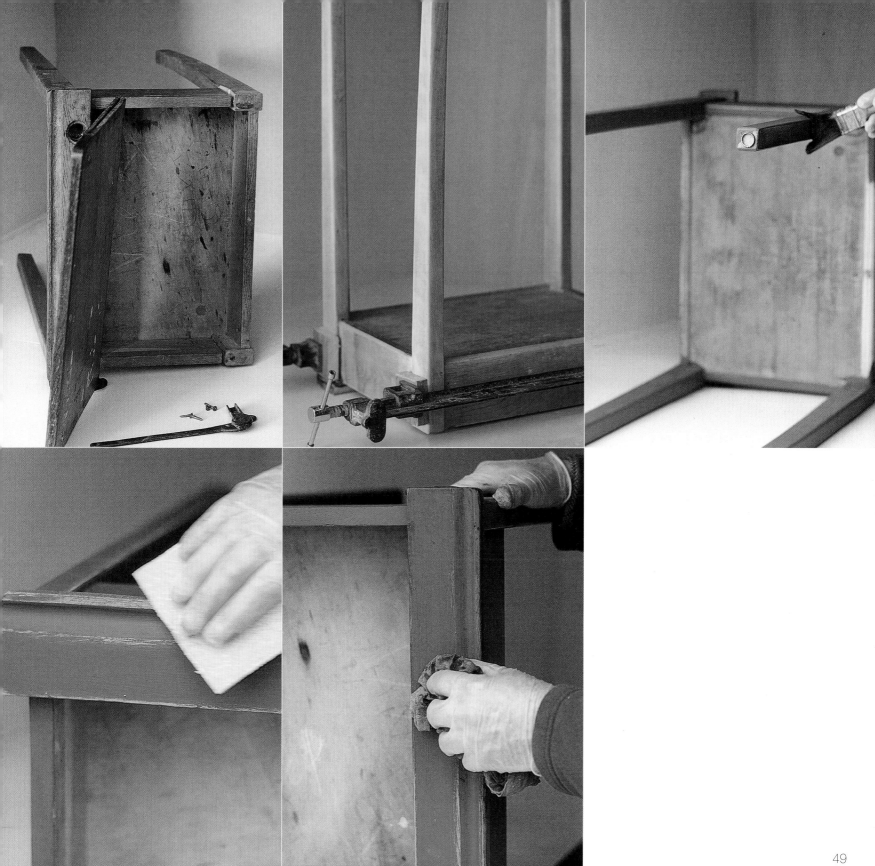

SLATE BOARD

EQUIPMENT

Paint scraper
Coarse metal file
Coarse-grade glasspaper
Medium- and fine-grade emery paper
38 mm (1½ in) paintbrush (optional)
Electric hammer drill
Masonry drill bit
Screwdriver

MATERIALS

Old slate
Satin interior varnish or milk (optional)
Rawlplugs
Two 50 mm (2 in) screws
Two washers to fit screws (optional)
Chalk or slate pencil

METHOD

1 Select an old slate in relatively good condition with regular edges and nail holes that are not too enlarged. Place the slate on a protected work area and prise off any loose delaminated slate or flaking with a paint scraper. Gently tap the surface of the slate with your knuckle; if you hear a hollow sound, more surface slate will have to be removed. Continue until you reveal a solid surface. Use the coarse metal file to clean the edges of the slate and remove any irregularities, always filing towards the edge of the slate.

2 When you have cleaned the slate as best you can with the paint scraper and coarse file, place it on your work area with the bevel-edged side up and use coarse glasspaper to smooth the surface to a rough finish. Complete the process with wetted medium-grade, followed by fine-grade, emery paper.

Wash the slate down with clean water and allow it to dry. If desired, the slate can be painted with one coat of satin interior varnish. Alternatively, follow the old Welsh tradition and apply a thin coat of milk to one surface. When dry, the milk seals the slate and provides an excellent, slightly shiny finish.

3 To fix the slate board to a wall, hold it against the wall in the desired position and mark the screw holes. Drill into the wall with the drill and masonry bit, insert rawlplugs and fit the slate board to the wall with screws driven through the nail holes into the rawlplugged holes. If the nail holes are a little large, place a washer behind the head of each screw before securing the slate to the wall. Write messages, or draw fanciful pictures, whatever your whim, on the fitted slate board with chalk or a slate pencil. A useful hint when using chalk is to wet it before use: when dry, the image or writing will stand out much better.

Safety note

Rubber or protective gloves are recommended for this project.

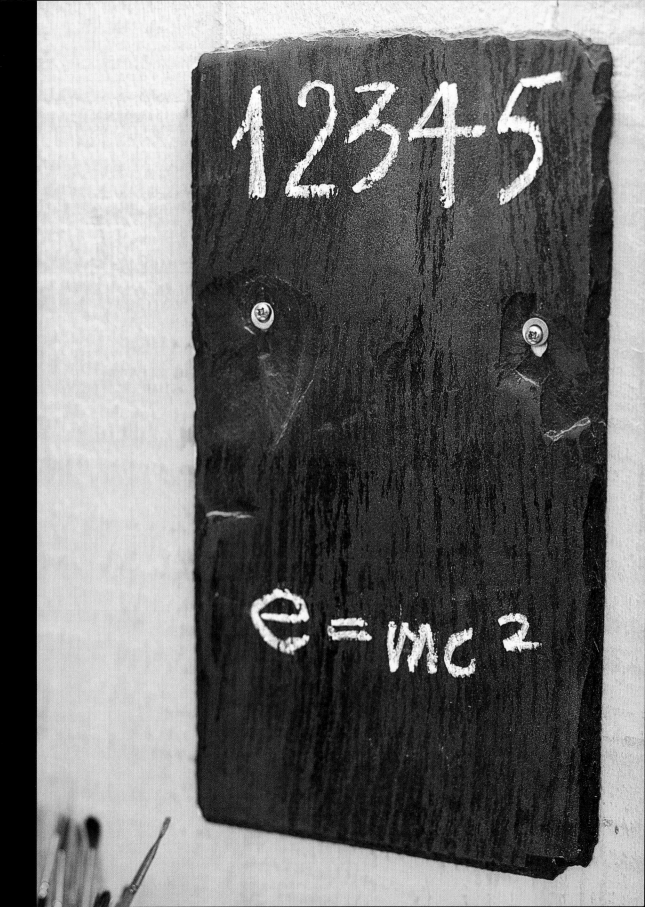

Before the days of inexpensively mass-produced paper, schoolchildren wrote their daily lessons on slate boards. Slate was readily available and economical, and had the added advantage that, after use, it could be wiped clean and used again. In some less wealthy countries slate boards are still in use in impoverished schools.

Slate is mined in many parts of the world and ranges in colour from almost black, through green and blue to palest grey. The slate we have used for this stylish wall-mounted board is from Wales, mined more than fifty years ago and removed from the roof of a house undergoing restoration. Almost all roofing slates are hand split and shaped to size; the nail holes are generally made at the time the slate is fitted to a roof, but all slates, whether old or new, show evidence on their face of the splitter's blow. All hand-split slates have one flat face and one with a bevelled edge.

We have used the existing nail holes in this slate to fit it to the wall. With a little effort, any slate can be easily transformed into a slick and functional wall display.

STORAGE RACK

EQUIPMENT

Stiff wire brush
Coarse-grade wire wool
Electric hammer drill
Masonry drill bit
Screwdriver

MATERIALS

Galvanised wire letter basket
Four rawlpugs
Four 38 mm (1½ in) screws

Safety note

Rubber or protective gloves are
recommended for this project.

METHOD

1 Make sure that the basket is dry and remove
any remains of protective tape or packaging
that might remain on it.

2 Clean the basket thoroughly with the stiff
wire brush then finish with the wire wool to
remove any residual oxidation or dirt.

When you are satisfied with the appearance of
your basket, hold it up to the wall in the desired
position, mark the fixing holes with a pencil, then
drill the pencil-marked holes with the electric drill
and masonry bit. Insert the rawlplugs before
fixing the rack to the wall with the 38 mm (1½ in)
screws.

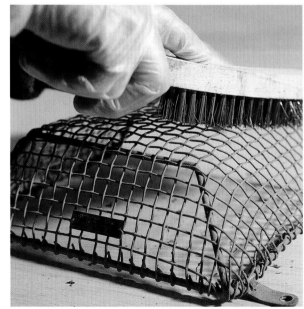

easy answer to a constant
storage problem – what to do with
books, papers and all those other
items that need to be close to
hand but can clutter up the
surface of a desk or table. A shelf
is not always practicable and
offers none of the advantages of
the kind of storage that allows
you to see instantly what is
stored. A wall-mounted rack,
however, offers useful vertical
storage for any room in the house.
We located these woven,
galvanised wire letter baskets in
one of our favourite hunting
grounds – government surplus
yards. Made half a century ago for
installation behind the doors of
army married quarters, they had
never been installed but were sold
off and ignored until we found
them. They had been stored out
of doors, but the heavy
galvanising had protected them
from the degradation of years of
exposure to the elements. Once
retrieved and the remnants of the
protective tape and brown paper
packaging removed, they were
almost as good as new.
We hope that this project will
encourage you to look at
unfamiliar objects with an open
mind, because part of the
enjoyment of working with
salvaged materials is trying to
think of new applications for
them. When we first discovered
these baskets, we thought that
they were too good to miss
although at the time we had no
idea of what we might use them
for. Once cleaned up, they have
proved to be indispensable in
helping to organise our office, the
kitchen and our teenage
daughter's bedroom.

SHUTTER CD RACK

EQUIPMENT

Screwdriver
Electric sander
Glasspaper
38 mm (1½ in) paintbrush
Soft cotton rag
Electric hammer drill
Masonry drill bit

MATERIALS

Old wooden window shutter
Colourless timber preservative
Wood filler (if necessary)
Two contrasting colours of matt emulsion
    paint
Satin finish interior wood varnish
Hardboard or thin plywood to fit the back
    of the shutter
Matt black emulsion paint
Small wood screws or panel pins
Two mirror plates
Rawlplugs
Screws to fit mirror plates

Safety note

We advise that you wear safety glasses or goggles
when using any mechanical sanding equipment; a
dust mask is also sensible in case the surface to be
sanded has been finished with a lead-based paint.
Rubber or protective gloves are also
recommended for this project.

We know from personal
experience that this shutter CD
rack is a good idea because it ha
a teenager's seal of approval.
Teenagers usually buy CDs more
frequently than the rest of us, and
as a collection of CDs expands
storage can become a problem.
    Of the innumerable CD storag
systems that are commercially
available, most take up valuable
surface space and few can be
described as well designed. If,
however, you are able to find an
old wooden louvre shutter, which
will undoubtedly need some
attention, if only a coat of paint,
we are sure you will agree that,
once wall mounted at eye-level
with the CD titles on view, it
provides the ideal storage solution
    When selecting an old wooden
shutter for conversion into a CD
rack, make sure to measure the
width of the slats and their
distance apart to ensure that the
finished rack will comfortably hold
boxed CDs. If you wish, you can
use the shutter in its original
condition and not repaint it, but if
it is to fit into an existing interior
scheme it is probably best to
paint it in the colour or colours of
your choice. We selected an old
shutter that showed considerable
evidence of age and wear and
decided to repaint it in two
contrasting colours, completing it
with a simulated aged and
distressed finish.

SHUTTER CD RACK

METHOD

1 Remove any hinges or other metal hardware, sand down any flaked and loose paint from the shutter and treat with colourless timber preservative. Fill any holes or damage with wood filler, wait for the filler to set then sand it down to match the surrounding timber. Sand the whole of the shutter to provide a smooth surface for repainting. It is not necessary to remove all the old paint, but pay particular attention to revealing the underlying timber on the edges of the frame and slats, where natural wear would occur.

2 When you are satisfied with the finish you have achieved, paint the shutter frame in the darker of your selected colours of emulsion paint and leave to dry. Then paint the slats in a contrasting paler colour and again leave to dry.

3 When the shutter is completely dry, sand through the surface of the paint to reveal the underlying wood on all the outside edges of the frame and the exposed edges of the slats. You can either use an electric sander or, for a more subtle effect, sand by hand. The sanding is designed to simulate natural wear; if you do make a mistake, it is very simple to repaint and start again.

4 When the frame is looking suitable distressed, clean off any dust with the cotton rag and apply two coats of satin finish interior wood varnish to the entire shutter, leaving it to dry between coats.

Cut the sheet of hardboard or thin plywood to fit approximately 12 mm (½ in) inside the reverse of the shutter. Paint one side with matt black emulsion and, when dry, attach it to the rear of the shutter with panel pins or screws. Fit two mirror plates to the rear of the shutter and decide on its hanging position. Drill the holes and insert rawlplugs before screwing the CD rack to the wall.

The ideal kitchen these days is very much a living room, sometimes large enough to cook, eat and socialise in, making it the centre of family life. The sitting room and perhaps a

ROOMS FOR LIVING

conservatory are also rooms where family and friends can gather for informal entertaining, in tune with the more casual, relaxed lifestyle that many of us now choose.

The decor and the objects we display make a strong statement reflecting our personalities, and with the eclectic nature of decorating today, nothing is totally predictable. Mix surreal combinations of furniture and colours – that is half the fun of decorating. A favourite picture or object that costs next to nothing does not have to be taken too seriously, because it injects an individuality and freshness into a scheme that can easily be changed with the next new idea.

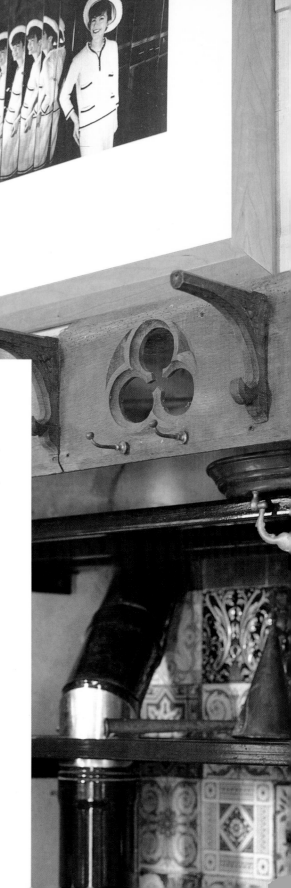

Salvage ideas for these living rooms include vintage office furniture, mass-produced between the 1930s and the 1960s, much of it made of steel or wood or a combination of both to be functional, durable and well designed. Now, after years of neglect, it is being reclaimed and restored, the dull grey paint covered with vibrant colours to give it a new lease of life, a new purpose and a place in our homes. Another unconventional idea, from Spanish furniture designer Diego Fortunato, is to make a base from the cheapest industrial metal shelving, once used to store plans, and to cover it with piles of huge, sumptuous velvet cushions in rich reds and purples, creating a stylish daybed.

These versatile pieces of furniture can be assimilated into any room, mixing comfortably with antiques, at a fraction of the price paid for similar styles from a designer range.

In complete contrast, if you have a liking for the warmth of wood looking naturally distressed, consider using old scaffold boards, disused railway sleepers, discarded fencing, floorboards and farmyard gates for making into large dining tables, coffee tables, benches, mirrors, picture frames and capacious cupboards. This rough-hewn, unrefined furniture celebrates its origins, revelling in the occasional evidence of woodworm, knots and scores in its often stained, battered and worn surfaces.

NEAR LEFT

A carved wooden fire surround, bought from a reclamation yard then gilded and fitted with glass, makes a superb over-mantle mirror above a drawing-room fireplace.

BOTTOM RIGHT

A decorative over-mantle has been painted and placed above a shelf in a laundry room to deflect the eye from the utilitarian boiler below.

BOTTOM LEFT

The unusual door was cut down and made to fit the opening to what was once the vestry of this converted church. The stone kitchen sink, taps and marble-top butcher's slab all came from a reclamation yard. The owner of the church once taught art courses, and the large plate seen behind the taps was a present from a ceramics student.

FAR LEFT

Cast-iron nineteenth-century pillars salvaged from a Baptist chapel make an elegant feature installed behind plate glass doors which lead on to a flag-stoned terrace and the well-managed garden beyond.

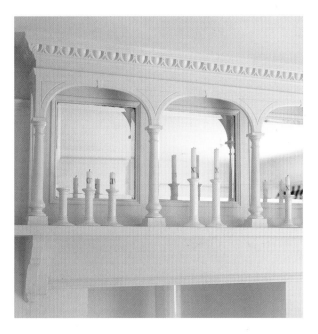

LEFT

The rack above the cooking range was at one time used to hang cassocks in the vestry, and the Victorian tiles were amassed over a period of twenty or thirty years by Angela Coombes, the owner of this converted church. The evocative framed photograph by Norman Parkinson was taken for *Queen* magazine in the Chanel showroom, Paris, in the early 1960s; it is part of the Angela Coombes archive collection.

SLATE-TILED WALL

EQUIPMENT

Palette knife
Emery paper or emery cloth
Tape measure
Diamond-blade electric tile cutter
Slate cutter (optional)
50 mm (2 in) paintbrush
Spirit level
Chalk
Tile adhesive spreader
Cotton rag
Fine artist's paintbrush

MATERIALS

Selection of old roofing slates
Black matt emulsion paint
Wall tile adhesive
Satin finish interior or floor varnish

Safety note

Electrical cutting equipment can be dangerous. Most electric tile cutters use water as a coolant and create a great deal of spray. You are advised to wear safety goggles if using any electrical cutter, and gloves and protective clothes are advisable if you use a water-cooled tile cutter.

Slate, limestone, terracotta and marble are immensely popular natural wall and floor coverings in both domestic and commercial environments, despite strong competition from modern man-made high-tech materials.

Hard-wearing slate has long been admired for its beauty as well as its durability. It comes in wonderful shades of red and heather blue as well as the classic dark blue-grey which seems to go with everything and has always been a favourite material for floors, kitchen worktops and wall cladding. A mix of slate with limestone, marble or terracotta is very much in vogue. Despite the fact that they are a fraction of the thickness of traditional flooring slate and have a tendency to flake, reclaimed roofing slates can be used very successfully on floors if laid on a bed of cement to give them a solid base. Floor tiles were often sealed with a coat of milk or oil in the days before pre-prepared sealants became readily available.

Select your old roofing slates for condition. Ideally those you use for this project should be fairly regular in thickness, free of too much flaking (delamination), of similar colour and should have two reasonably undamaged edges. If the tiles are in particularly good condition, there may be no need to cut them down, but most reclaimed slates have at least one edge damaged and the nail fixing holes have enlarged due to the passage of time and the enthusiasm with which they were removed from the roof.

SLATE-TILED WALL

METHOD

If the slates you will be using for this project are delaminating, it is a good idea to prise off the loose layers with a palette knife or similar blade until you have revealed a sound surface. This surface can be cleaned with emery paper or wetted emery cloth to produce a smooth finish.

Measure your tiles and decide on a size into which the tiles can be economically cut. This size should ensure that the cut slate will not include any unsightly nail holes and that the width will be trimmed to lose any damaged edge. For simplicity, we chose to cut our slates into squares, which has the advantage that cutting on the diamond-bladed tile cutter is accomplished in two passes with no need to change the saw fence setting.

Slates cut in this fashion will have two straight cut edges and two of the original naturally bevelled edges. For a really professional finish, you should make the first two cuts of the slate about 25 mm (1 in) larger than the required dimension, then reduce the saw fence measurement and pass the slates through the saw for a third and fourth time, trimming off the bevelled edges to give four neatly cut edges.

It is perfectly possible to cut the slates for this project with a slate cutter (see the Slate Table Mats project in the chapter Wining and Dining), but the resulting edges may not allow the cut slates to be butted neatly together.

1 Measure the area you will be tiling with the cut slates and work out the number required. Remember to provide for areas where slates will need to be cut to shape or where part-slates will be required for edges or ends of runs. We suggest that you cut a number of extra slates to provide for inevitable breakages.

Start the diamond-blade tile cutter and make sure that the water reservoir is full and that the spinning blade produces a fine spray of water to both lubricate and cool the slate when it is being cut. Set the fence to the desired width, hold the slate firmly in both hands and, with the true edge against the fence, pass it across the saw table until cut through. Turn the slate through 90 degrees and make a second cut at right angles to the first to produce a square slate with two cut and two bevelled edges. Repeat until you have as many slates as you require.

2 Carefully mark out the area you will be tiling and paint it with one or two coats of matt black emulsion paint. When the paint is dry, mark the central point on the width of the area to be tiled and, using a spirit level for accuracy, draw a line from the floor to the top of the area with chalk. Calculate how many horizontal rows of slates will be required to tile the area, halve that number and multiply by the dimension of the cut slates. Measure down from the top of the area to be tiled by this amount, and at that point draw a second and horizontal line crossing the first and stretching from one side of the area to the other.

3 Begin by fixing the slates as vertical and horizontal rows abutting the chalk marks, leaving a matchstick width between. Apply wall tile adhesive with the spreader to the back of a slate, then press it firmly on to the wall with a gentle twisting movement. Remove any excess adhesive with a damp cloth. For best results, as far as possible try to fit cut edge against cut edge and bevelled edge against bevelled edge. When you have fitted the slates to the chalk lines, commence filling in the remaining area with further slates, using the first rows as a guide, until the wall is covered. Periodically check your work with the spirit level and tape measure.

4 Use the slate cutter or the diamond-bladed tile cutter to trim slates to fit round awkward areas and where half- or part-slates are required. Use a moist rag to remove any spilled adhesive and wipe over the surface of the slates to remove any last residues of dirt or dust. When the adhesive is completely dry, use the fine artist's brush dipped in the black matt emulsion paint to touch up as required. Apply at least two coats of satin finish interior or floor varnish (the floor varnish is somewhat harder wearing), leaving the wall to dry between coats. Pay particular attention to covering those areas between the slates where the black paint is revealed.

To maintain the appearance of your slate-tiled wall, periodically wipe it over with a damp cloth. If the finish deteriorates, it can be restored with a further application of varnish.

WAISTED CUPBOARD

EQUIPMENT

Bench saw or band saw
Tape measure
Set square
Hammer
Electric jigsaw
Saucer
Electric sander
Glasspaper
Electric drill and drill bit
Screwdriver
25 mm (1 in) paintbrush
Waxing brush or stiff-bristled paintbrush
Soft polishing brush
Lint-free cotton rag

MATERIALS

Waterproof wood glue
38 mm (1½ in) annular ring nails
38 mm (1½ in) panel pins
25 mm (1 in) panel pins
Mid-brown wood stain
Four 75 mm (3 in) screws
Antique brown furniture wax
18 mm (¾ in) brass screws
Two 65 mm (2½ in) brass Parliament or butt
    hinges
13 cm (5 in) brass pull handle
40 mm (1⅝ in) brass turn button
25 mm (1 in) brass screw and washer

TIMBER

For the sides:
Four boards approx. 89 cm x 11 cm x
    12 mm (35 x 4¼ x ½ in)

For the shelves:
Three pieces of floorboard approx. 22 cm x
    22 mm (8½ x ⅞ in), one cut to 28 cm
    (11 in) and two cut to 30 cm (12 in)

For the back:
Four boards approx. 89 cm x 9 cm x 15 mm
    (35 x 3½ x ⅝ in)

For the front:
Two boards approx. 89 cm x 9 cm x 15 mm
    (35 x 3½ x ⅝ in)
One top piece approx. 17 cm x 9 cm x
    15 mm (6½ x 3½ x ⅝ in)
One bottom piece approx. 17 cm x 12.5 cm
    x 15 mm (6½ x 5 x ⅝ in)

For the door:
Two boards approx. 63 cm x 85 mm x
    15 mm (24¾ x 3¼ x ⅝ in)
Two braces approx. 17 cm x 10 cm x
    15 mm (6½ x 4 x ⅝ in)
Two pieces approx. 17 cm x 15 mm x
    15 mm (6½ x ⅝ x ⅝ in)

For the top:
Two pieces to make approx. 38 x 26 x 5 cm
    (15 x 10¼ x 2 in)

Other:
You will also need a number of pieces of
waste timber for bracing and supporting
the joints.

If you are looking for furniture or storage ideas with some individuality – something a little different from the mass-produced designs of the high street – try making our rustic-looking 'waisted' cupboard. This highly unusual, 'semi-rough' cupboard can be made in all sorts of sizes, and we have made a very successful taller version. It was constructed using timber salvaged from horticultural and produce boxes, some with the original stencil marking intact, imported from the Netherlands into Britain before the use of lighter-weight cardboard and plastic containers. Had it not been rescued, this timber would have been used for firewood.

Select different thicknesses of wood for the construction: thin for the sides without knots (to allow for uniform bending into the 'waist' shape), thicker for the doors, front and back, and thicker still for the interior shelves. Any piece of waste timber can be used for the top of the cupboard, as long as it is fairly chunky. We cut our front, door and sides from the framework of the horticultural boxes, whilst the sides were made from the thinner cladding. The shelves were sawn from an old floorboard and the top was cut from two pieces of old floor joist, glued together to create a piece of the required width. We waxed the finished piece and used 'aged' brass door fittings, but it could also be given a very effective naturally distressed limed look and fitted with old steel hinges, handle and turn button.

WAISTED CUPBOARD

METHOD

This project demonstrates how to make a waisted cupboard measuring approximately 94 cm (37 in) high x 26 cm (10¼ in) deep and 38 cm (15 in) wide. All measurements can be adjusted to make a cupboard of a different size.

1 Cut the four pieces of timber cut the sides of the cupboard, making sure that there are few knots in the timber, and measure three points 75 mm (3 in), 42 cm (16½ in) and 76 cm (30 in) from one end (the top). Use the set square and a pencil to mark lines at these points across the width of the boards. Apply wood glue to the ends of the three shelves and nail them to the side pieces at these points, using the 38 mm (1½ in) annular ring nails to hold the joints securely. The 28 cm (11 in) shelf should be nailed at the 42 cm (16½ in) point to form the middle shelf.

2 Turn the assembled framework on to its front, keeping the unsawn and naturally coloured edge of the shelves facing the front of the cupboard, then, with a pencil, mark a point at the exact centre of the width of each shelf. Apply wood glue to approximately the central 18 cm (7 in) of the rear of each shelf and use 38 mm (1½ in) panel pins to secure one of the four back boards to the shelves so that one edge exactly abuts each marked centre point. (This will ensure that the curved sides match.) Place a second board abutting and outside the first one, and secure it lightly in place with just one or two 25 mm (1 in) panel pins.

3 Attach the third and fourth back boards in the same way to the opposite side of the centre marks. Turn the frame over so that the back of the cupboard is underneath and the extra width of the newly fitted boards can be seen protruding from under the curved edges. With a pencil, draw the shape of the curve on these boards, again turn the frame over, remove the loosely fitted two outside boards and extract the panel pins used to fit them temporarily in place.

4 Place the two removed boards on a solid work surface and cut out the pencil-marked curve with the jigsaw. Apply wood glue to the rear of the shelves and fit the two cut-out back boards in position with 38 mm (1½ in) panel pins.

5 Turn the cupboard on to its back and mark the shelf centres on the front with a pencil. Mark a point 85 mm (3¼ in) away on either side of these centre marks on each shelf. Place one of the 89 cm (35 in) front boards abutting the outside of these points and secure it with one or two 25 mm (1 in) panel pins. Turn the cupboard over, mark the curve with a pencil, remove the board and cut out the shape with the jigsaw. Apply wood glue to the front of the shelves where the board was placed and fit in position with 38 mm (1½ in) panel pins. Repeat with the second front board.

6 Take the 17 cm x 9 cm x 15 mm (6½ x 3½ x ⅝ in) front top piece, apply glue to the sides and the exposed edge of the top shelf of the cupboard, then nail the top piece securely in place between the curved front boards with 38 mm (1½ in) panel pins, its top flush with the top of the cupboard. (It may be necessary to support this piece with scrap timber glued and nailed with 25 mm/1 in panel pins behind the curved front boards.) The 17 cm x 12.5 cm x 15 mm (6½ x 5 x ⅝ in) front bottom piece should be fitted to the bottom of the cupboard between the curved front boards, supported by scrap timber glued and nailed from behind with 25 mm (1 in) panel pins. When the glue has dried, place a saucer or similar circular shape at the base of the fitted bottom piece, draw round the curve with a pencil ánd cut out with the jigsaw.

7 Use the electric sander and glasspaper to smooth off all irregularities, sharp corners and rough timber. Stain any sawn edges with mid-brown wood stain, diluted to match the existing weathered timber. Measure the door space you have created and put the cupboard to one side. Take the two 63 cm (24¾ in) door boards and join them together with the two 17 cm (6½ in) braces fitted across the rear and fixed with wood glue and 25 mm (1 in) panel pins. Take the two 17 cm (6½ in) pieces of 15 mm (⅝ in) square timber, glue one side and fit one each to the top and bottom of the door with 38 mm (1½ in) panel pins. This will help to prevent the door cupping (distorting). Place the assembled door in position and shape with the electric sander to fit it loosely in place.

8 Glue and nail four pieces of waste timber above the top shelf, inside and flush with the top of the cupboard, to provide a base into which the screws used to fit the top will be fixed. When the glue is dry, apply more wood glue to the top of the waste timber and place the two pieces forming the top in place, the back flush with the rear of the cupboard and with an equal overhang on each side. Drill four holes through the top into the waste timber underneath and fix in place with 75 mm (3 in) screws.

Use the waxing brush or soft-bristled paintbrush to apply antique brown furniture wax to the door, top, front and sides of the cupboard. When it is dry, polish with the soft brush and lint-free cotton rag. Use the 18 mm (¾ in) brass screws to fit the brass hinges to the door, centred 15 cm (6 in) from the top and bottom. Finally, attach the brass pull handle and fit the turn button outside the door with a 25 mm (1 in) brass screw and a washer underneath, positioned so that it will secure the door when closed.

CURTAIN POLE AND CURTAINS

EQUIPMENT

Tape measure
Hacksaw or pipe cutter
Paint stripper
Old paintbrush
Offcut of waste timber
Cotton rag
Craft knife
Glasspaper
Electric hammer drill
Masonry drill bit
Screwdriver

MATERIALS

Length of 25/28 mm (metric) copper tubing
Approx. 30 cm (12 in) broom handle
Two tent pole finials or similar decorative
     finials
Wood glue
Four brass 28 mm (metric) Munson rings
Four rawlplugs
Four 50 mm (2 in) screws
Clip-on brass curtain rings
Two antique linen sheets

Safety note

Paint stripper is extremely caustic; rubber or
protective gloves and eye protection are essential
for this project.

It is so simple and inexpensive to make a curtain pole, given some old copper piping, two wooden tent pole finials and a few other bits and pieces, that you may decide never to buy one again. Just think of the savings if you were you to make them for the whole house!

Copper piping develops colour and patination with age even when the metal is hidden behind layers of paint. It can be bought second-hand from a waste metal merchant who will probably charge you for the scrap value only. Copper pipe can be found in various gauges and we chose 25/28mm (metric) for our curtain pole, a gauge often still used in internal pipe work.

To fix the pipe to the wall we used Munson rings, which are purpose-made for pipe fixing. They are manufactured in two parts: the bracket has two screw holes to allow it to be fixed to the wall, whilst the outer part which screws into the bracket comprises two semi-circular holders which secure the pipe. Munson rings are readily available, inexpensive and provide a practical alternative to curtain brackets.

The metal pipe and wood fittings combine well for the casual, unsophisticated look we were aiming for. We teamed the pole with simple curtains of heavy antique cream linen. Essentially utilitarian, sometimes embroidered with initials in red and occasionally fringed, they were used as sheets in French farmhouses in the early 1900s. Those we used were particularly long and had one embroidered and tasselled end. We chose to make a feature of this by folding and hanging them so that the embroidery could be seen.

CURTAIN POLE AND CURTAINS

METHOD

1 Measure the width of the window opening for which the curtain pole is being made. Add approximately 20 cm (8 in) at each end, then cut the copper tube to that dimension with a pipe cutter or hacksaw. If the pipe is painted, strip the paint with chemical paint stripper. Follow the manufacturer's instructions carefully and use protective gloves, eye protection and wear an apron or old clothes when doing this. Lay the pipe on a disposable surface and apply the stripper liberally to the painted surface with an old paintbrush. Leave for a short while until the paint blisters, then start to remove the softened paint with a scrap of waste wood. Do not use a metal scraper or anything else that is likely to scratch the surface of the pipe and so remove the patination that has developed over time. Repeat the process as many times as is necessary to remove all the paint, wiping the pipe clean with cotton rag between applications.

2 When the pipe is clean, wash it down with soapy water, dry with clean cotton rag and place to one side. Cut the broom handle into two halves with the hacksaw. Using the craft knife and glasspaper, shape and sand down an end of one until it fits tightly into one of the tent pole finials. Fit the other piece of broom handle into the second finial in the same way. Use the craft knife and glasspaper to shape and sand the other ends: one finial should fit tightly into the pipe, whilst the other should be sanded so that it is slightly loose and can be easily removed to allow the curtain rings to be fitted over the pipe.

3 Place the completed curtain pole against and above the window in the desired position and mark where the supports should be fitted. These should be placed at both ends of the pole and just outside the window opening, leaving an approximately 15 cm (6 in) overhang at each end. Unscrew the Munson rings from their brackets, place the brackets at the selected points on the wall and mark the screw holes with a pencil. Drill out holes in the wall at the marked points with the electric drill and masonry bit to a depth of approximately 50 mm (2 in), insert the rawlplugs and fit the Munson ring brackets with the four 50 mm (2 in) screws.
    Unscrew the two semi-circular Munson ring holders and attach the halves with the threaded attachment to the brackets fixed to the wall.

4 Remove the loose finial from one end of the pole, thread the curtain rings on to it and replace the finial. Offer up the pole to the half Munson rings attached to the brackets and secure it in place with the previously removed half-rings. Check that the pole is centred on the brackets and, importantly, that one curtain ring is positioned outside the bracket but inside the finial on each side. Secure in place, tightening the Munson ring bolts with the screwdriver.
    Fold the sheets so that, when hung, they will drop to the ground. Divide the curtain rings in two, push half to each end of the pole for each curtain and clip them on to the folded material at regular intervals. The last ring on each side, positioned outside the bracket, will keep the curtains spread when they are pulled across the window.

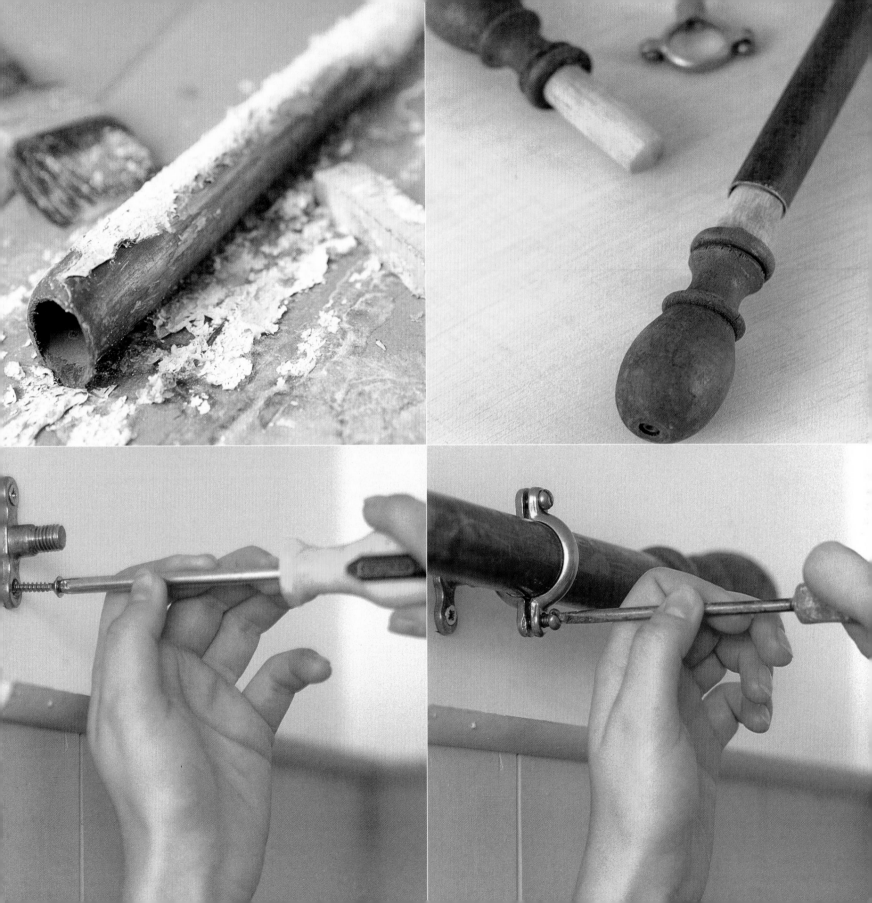

SEA DEFENCE COFFEE TABLE

EQUIPMENT

Angle grinder and sanding disc attachment
Orbital electric sander
Waxing brush or stiff-bristled paintbrush
Lint-free cotton rag
Kitchen paper (optional)

MATERIALS

Three wood blocks
Dark brown furniture wax
Glass round at least 12 mm (½ in) thick
Glass cleaner

METHOD

1 Select three blocks that match in appearance and height. If the ends are not level, they should be sawn or sanded to shape. Place one of the wooden blocks on a flat work surface covered with a disposable surface. Use the angle grinder to grind off any surface irregularities and heavy saw marks and finish to a smooth surface with the orbital sander.

2 Apply a liberal quantity of dark brown furniture wax to the sides and top of the block with the waxing or stiff-bristled brush. Rub the wax well into the surface with the soft cotton rag to accentuate the grain and colour of the timber; rub off any excess and leave it to dry. Be careful not to apply any wax to the base of the block because this will mark the floor when the coffee table is installed.

3 Polish with some lint-free cotton rag, using a new cloth when the first is soiled. For best results, polishing should be done in a figure of eight motion, which should leave no smears or marks on the surface of the wood. Be careful to remove any surface wax from the sawn surface of the top of the block because this might mark the glass top. Again, check the base of the block for any wax residue.

Place the three blocks carefully in the place where you propose to install the coffee table. The blocks should be placed an equal distance from each other and so that their tops will be approximately 20 cm (8 in) from the outside edge of the glass when it is placed on top. Clean the glass with glass cleaner, polishing it with more lint-free cotton rag or absorbent kitchen paper, and, when you are satisfied with the result, gently place the glass in position on the blocks.

Safety note

When using an angle grinder it is advisable to use safety glasses or goggles and a dust mask. A dust mask should always be used when sanding with an electric sander. Rubber or protective gloves are also recommended for this project.

hen our eyes first alighted on
e massive wooden blocks cut
om the tapered ends of old oak
ea defence supports, we were
mediately drawn to their size
nd strength. These timbers, lifted
om the sea bed when the
efences were renewed, were
scued by John Tyler of JAT
eclamation, who cut them into
eams and lintels, leaving behind
e tapered ends which we
scovered in his yard.
  Years of exposure to salt water
ad hardened and darkened the
ak, which had also been
scoloured by the iron nails
riven in to fix the steel caps
at once protected them.
  We felt strongly that these
unks of raw timber could be
rned into something exciting
nd innovative, and decided on a
esign for a coffee table using the
osts for legs. By chance, we
ame across a huge salvaged
ound of glass, so heavy that it
ok two men to lift it. The origins
f this junk shop find were
nknown, but our hunch was that
had previously been used as a
ble top, suffering remarkably
w scratches. The combination
f gleaming glass and natural
arm, tactile wood gave us
xactly the clean architectural
es and interesting contours we
ad envisaged.
  Any timber blocks could be
sed to make a similar table, or
ou may wish to construct the
gs from terracotta pipes, lumps
f stone or even concrete blocks.

SEA DEFENCE LAMP

Rough-hewn and shaped like obelisks, these mighty, metal-braced, oak sea defence posts, once driven deep into the tidal sands to support the palisades that protect the coast from sea erosion, were a truly exciting discovery. Because of their singularity, we felt that they were more than worthy of two differen treatments. In this project, one has been made into a lamp with something of an oriental feel, an the shade reinforces the shape c the rich, dark, heavy base. The alternative project (Sea Defence Coffee Table on the previous pages) uses three posts as gargantuan legs for an ethnically stylish glass-topped coffee table

EQUIPMENT

Electric drill
12 mm (½ in) spade or auger bit
Drill bit extension bar
Poker (optional)
Tenon saw
12 mm (½ in) wood chisel
Hacksaw
Metal file
Palette knife
Electrician's screwdriver
Stiff-bristled brush (optional)
Soft cotton rag (optional)

MATERIALS

Oak post or other large block of wood
30 cm (12 in) of 10 mm (metric)
    threaded brass batten
Threaded brass lamp holder
Threaded brass adaptor (optional)
Two-part epoxy putty
Approx. 20 cm (8 in) of 15 mm (⅝ in)
    copper tube
Fused electric plug
Three-wire lamp cord
Brown sealant or filler
Antique brown furniture wax (optional)
Lampshade cradle
Electric light bulb
Lampshade

Safety note

Electricity is potentially dangerous; we suggest you get a qualified and experienced electrician to check any electrical work you undertake for this project. Since a metal lamp fitting is used for this lamp, it is most important that three-wire lamp cord is used and that the earth wire is connected both to the lamp holder and the fused electrical plug.

SEA DEFENCE LAMP

METHOD

1 Place the wooden block on a flat surface, mark the centre point on the top surface and drill a hole to the maximum depth possible, making sure the electric drill is held vertically. Either remove the drill, attach the bit to an extension bar and continue drilling until you have drilled through to the bottom of the block, or turn the block over and drill from the base to meet the hole drilled from the top.

2 Should you choose to drill from each end and the holes do not quite meet, or you need to deepen a drilled hole, you can heat a poker until its tip is red hot and use it to burn through the remaining timber. This may require several applications of the poker and will create considerable smoke. We suggest that you undertake this job out of doors and make sure that the block does not catch fire. Have some water handy.

3 Use the tenon saw to make two cuts approximately 12 mm ($\frac{1}{2}$ in) apart and 12 mm ($\frac{1}{2}$ in) deep on the base of the block from the central hole to an outside edge. Chisel out the waste to form a groove for the lamp cord. Place the length of 10 mm threaded batten in a vice or on a bench hook and cut it to length with a hacksaw. Clean the cut end with a metal file and test that it will thread easily on to the lamp holder. Depending on the thread gauges of the batten and lamp holder used, it may be necessary to join them with a threaded brass adapter.

4 Insert the batten into the hole cut through the wooden block, securing it in place with two-part epoxy putty or a similar filler or glue. Make sure that the batten is vertical in the hole and that no putty will prevent the lamp cord being threaded through the batten and through the hole drilled in the block. Use a palette knife to clean the top of the block of any putty squeezed out when the batten was inserted, then put the block to one side for the putty to harden.

5 Screw the lamp holder on to the batten. Measure from the top of the block to the base of the lamp holder and cut the 15 mm ($\frac{5}{8}$ in) copper tube to that length. Unscrew the lamp holder. Fit a fused electric plug to one end of the lamp cord, place the copper tube over the batten to form a sleeve, then pass the free end of the cord up through the base of the wooden block and through the batten until it emerges from the top. Fit the cord to the lamp holder with an electrician's screwdriver, then pull it back through the block until the lamp holder sits on top of the batten and copper pipe. Screw the lamp holder back on to the batten, securing the copper pipe sleeve in position.

Use the brown sealant or filler to secure the lamp cord into the groove cut into the base of the block. At this point, the lamp base may be waxed with antique brown furniture wax applied with the stiff-bristled brush, rubbed into the wood with soft cotton rag and polished off with more rag. Fit a lampshade frame on to the collar of the lamp holder, insert a light bulb and place your selected lampshade on the frame.

As we start the new millennium with a softer look, a more gentle kind of minimalism, we use decorative accessories to add impact and interest. Pottery, paintings, porcelain, cushions, less-worn areas of an old rug can be cut up and backed with sacking material to make enormous floor cushions or wall hangings, and the offcuts can be used for smaller cushions.

DECORATIVE ACCESSORIES

rugs and cherished collections that have evolved over time are the clever touches that transform a furnished house into a warm, welcoming and comfortable home. Not all decorative accessories need be expensive, and when you are bored with something cheap and cheerful, the look can easily be changed.

Textiles bring life and colour to a room. Use large throws and rugs, especially vegetable-dyed kilims in soft natural shades. The

Antique quilt covers, faded linens and silk saris, fabrics and colours in exquisite textures can be mixed to give a vibrant new look to jaded interiors. Visit jumble sales and bric-à-brac shops or raid the attic to find tapestries and beautiful brocades that were once much-loved curtains or ball gowns, which you can cut up to create sumptuous soft furnishings. Salvage old embroideries, braids, trimmings, fringes and ribbons for added decoration.

LEFT

Broken pieces of china and odd cup handles make up this vibrant mosaic vase, which is an early piece by Candace Bahouth.

RIGHT

This display of kitchen utensils, including various food graters collected from all over Europe, makes a focal point that is decorative as well as practical.

FAR RIGHT

Too worn for everyday use, these vegetable-dyed kilims have been salvaged and turned into beautiful floor cushions, their subtle colours blending with existing furnishings.

We show comfortable cushions made from old velvet curtains in delicious jewel-like colours with contrast piping, and the same vibrant colours used to recover outdated ottomans, finished off with a silk tassel.

Plain walls can be effectively decorated with framed pictures skilfully hung. Old floorboard timbers and disused scaffold boards are an obvious choice to make mirror or picture frames, the larger they are the more dramatic the effect. Do not dismiss the subtle black/brown tar finish of salvaged shiplap timber, disfigured and rotting former fencing posts or abandoned five-bar farm gates. Even prickly hedgerow twigs, berries and small boughs, glued together on to a small wooden frame and painstakingly gilded, make the most imaginative of frames.

Slate roofing tiles can be cut to suitable sizes to make frames or table mats, and discarded decorative windows, once a source of light and ventilation, can be transformed into unusual and imaginative mirrors by removing the panes and making use of the frames. Next time you dig the garden, start collecting all those fragments of pretty broken china found buried beneath the surface and turn them into a mosaic table top or cover a small shelf, an urn or a lamp base. A visit to the beach could be the start of a shell or pebble collection to cover small items like frames or boxes, turning them into intriguing decorative accessories.

Metals of different descriptions, from blackened iron curtain poles to the gleaming modernity of zinc, have been enjoying an

upsurge in popularity for the past few years. Metal looks good on its own but mixes equally well with the natural textures of wood, stone, slate and terracotta. It is often used in kitchens and bathrooms because of its hardwearing and practical qualities, but it should not be excluded from other rooms in the house. Tin plate is an inexpensive alternative to zinc with a strong contemporary look. So hunt out old catering tins: cleaned up, they can easily and inexpensively be adapted to make attractive, gleaming window boxes for herbs or flowers.

Books that are read and enjoyed give a home a lived-in, comfortable feel, and vases of freshly cut flowers, admired for their sweet-smelling scent as much as their beauty, can fill every room in the house.

LEFT

A glorious flight of fancy from Porter Design. Hedgerow cuttings have been dried, hot-glued to a wooden frame, sprayed with gesso and finished with solid gold leaf.

BOTTOM LEFT

Rich velvet curtains have been made into cushions by Milo Design. Enough fabric was left to cover an old ottoman.

FAR LEFT

A mirror made from roofing slates screwed on to a plywood base shows how basic materials can be given a new lease of life.

TONGUE-AND-GROOVE CLOCK

EQUIPMENT

Tape measure
Handsaw
Craft knife (optional)
Glasspaper
Mitre saw
Electric drill
Drill bit to fit the housing nut on the
    clock shaft
Hammer
Pliers

MATERIALS

Selection of tongue-and-groove
    match-boarding
Square of 9 mm (⅜ in) or 12 mm (½ in)
    plywood
Wood glue
25 mm (1 in) panel pins
Length of rough-cut timber approx.
    50 x 12 mm (2 x ½ in)
Battery-driven clock
Battery

METHOD

1 Choose a variety of different coloured tongue-and-groove match-boarding for similarity in size and pattern. Remove the tongue from the selected boards with a handsaw or craft knife, and finish flush with the edge with glasspaper to match the opposite grooved side. To cut the equilateral triangular pieces for your clockface, measure the width of the board and make a mark that distance along one length of the board for each two pieces you wish to cut. Cut off one end of the board at the first mark with the 90 degree setting of the mitre saw, move the saw to the 45 degree position and cut out the triangle. When the first triangle is cut, move the saw back to the 90 degree setting, slide the board up to the next mark and cut out a second triangle. Continue until you have cut the number of triangles required. Repeat with the different coloured boards.

2 Arrange the cut triangles on a flat surface until you have created the pattern you think looks most attractive. Measure the outside dimensions and cut a square to that size from the 9 mm (⅜ in) or 12 mm (½ in) plywood. Apply wood glue to one face of the plywood and place the triangles on it in your chosen pattern.

Place a weight on top and put to one side to dry. When it is fully dry, place the clock face up on a piece of waste timber and drill a hole in the centre from the front through the boarding and plywood and into the waste wood underneath. Drilling through the face into waste wood minimises the risk of the hole tearing where the bit emerges.

3 Take the length of rough-cut timber and cut it on the mitre saw to fit as a frame around the clockface. Fix it in place with wood glue and 25 mm (1 in) panel pins driven into the plywood edges.

4 Fit the clock housing nut from the front into the hole drilled into the clockface, then insert the clock mechanism from the rear, passing the shaft up through the drilled hole into the housing nut. Attach the clock hands and secure with the locking nut tightened with pliers. Attach a battery to the reverse of the clock mechanism, adjust the hands to the correct time and hang your finished clock in place. If you wish, you can fit a strut to the rear of the clock and use it free-standing.

We much admired frames made from recycled tongue-and-groove cypress match-boarding on the stand of Laville Frames Inc. at a furniture trade fair in North Carolina. Thomas and Ursula Laville run a business in Baton Rouge, Louisiana, committed to 'ecological consciousness'. They make an ever-widening range of furniture from salvaged and recycled materials, including rusted corrugated iron, copper sheeting, pine skirting boards and other discarded timbers.

In this project we show how a simple clock can be constructed from readily sourced tongue-and-groove match-boarding.

Tongue-and-groove match-boarding has been produced in a multitude of sizes and patterns. Modern tongue-and-groove, sold as 'T&G', is generally about 100 mm (4 in) in width and 6 mm (¼ in) in thickness; older tongue-and-groove can be 15 cm (6 in), 20 cm (8 in) or even 23 cm (9 in) wide and is normally 12 mm (½ in) thick. Various patterns are available, the most common is tongue, groove and vee, or 'TG&V', and the most attractive is probably tongue, groove and bead, 'TG&Bead'. When butted together, the tongue of each board fits into the groove of its neighbour, and the vee or bead makes an attractive and uniform feature across the assembled boarding.

Much salvaged tongue-and-groove is damaged in the process of being dismantled, often having its tongue broken off, but since this project calls for the tongue to be removed anyway, this damaged timber, which can often be purchased quite cheaply, is fine.

FENCE FRAME

EQUIPMENT

Tape measure
Set square
Handsaw
Screwdriver
Medium-grade glasspaper
12 mm (½ in) paintbrush
Glass cleaner
Lint-free cotton rag or kitchen paper
Hammer
Electric hammer drill (optional)
Masonry drill bit (optional)

MATERIALS

Two 135 cm (53 in) lengths of 12 mm (½ in)
    thick fence timber, one 75 mm (3 in)
    wide and one 65 mm (2½ in) wide,
    selected for colour and condition
Colourless wood preservative
Wood glue
18 mm (¾ in) screws
Medium brown timber stain
Glass or mirror glass to fit frame rebate
Hardboard or 6 mm (¼ in) plywood to fit
    frame rebate
25 mm (1 in) panel pins
Two screw eyes or D rings
Picture hook or screw hook
Nylon picture cord

METHOD

1 Treat your fence timber lengths with the wood preservative. Use a set square and pencil to mark the 75 mm (3 in) length into two 45 cm (18 in) and two 20 cm (8 in) lengths. Cut to length with the handsaw and, selecting the better face of the timber to be the front, place face down on a flat surface, with the shorter lengths placed between the longer lengths in the shape of the frame you are constructing.

2 Measure the width of the assembled frame shape. The measurement should be approximately 35 cm (14 in). Cut two pieces from the 65 mm (2½ in) fence timber to this length. Apply wood glue to the back of the assembled frame, then place the new timbers over both widths, making sure the outside edges match. Fix each length in place with 18 mm (¾ in) screws, ensuring that they are driven into all three lengths of underlying timber. Measure the gap between the two newly fitted lengths – the measurement should be approximately 33 cm (13 in) – and cut two lengths to that size from the remaining 65 mm (2½ in) fence timber. Fit these lengths into place on the frame, securing them with 18 mm (¾ in) screws, again ensuring that the outside edges are flush.

3 When the glue is dry, turn the assembled frame over and use glasspaper to sand off any sharp edges. Apply the medium brown stain, diluted to match, to disguise all the exposed newly sawn timber. Cut the glass or mirror glass (or have it cut by a glazier) and the hardboard or plywood backing to fit the frame rebate (approximately 33 x 23 cm/13 x 9 in). Clean the glass or mirror glass. Place your selected image between the cleaned glass and the backing and insert it into the frame; secure with 25 mm (1 in) panel pins driven into the sides of the rebate. Alternatively, place the mirror into the frame rebate and secure in the same way.

Measure approximately one-third down from the top of the frame and insert the screw eyes or D rings in the centre of each side of the frame. Pass the nylon cord through both rings, bring to the centre and tie securely with a slip-proof knot. Your frame or mirror is now ready to hang.

Safety note

Remember always to use a wall fixing able to hold the weight of your frame. Smaller frames can be securely hung on single or double picture hooks which can be driven into most plaster or sold walls; heavier frames will need to be hung on a hook drilled and rawlplugged into the wall.

The wood used to frame this botanical print is rather appropriately taken from old garden fencing that had been dismantled and replaced. After years of battering from high winds, much had fallen down and some had rotted, but there was still an abundance of good solid wood that was reusable and consequently salvaged. Fencing is generally made from standard softwood but sometimes cedar is used, which has a natural resistance to rot. The uneven colour comes from exposure to the elements and the effects of lichens and fungi, which have attached themselves to the rough surface of the timber over the years.

Whether you are making mirror or picture frames, consider using reclaimed shiplap timber, old packing cases or pallets, all of which make interesting, unusual and inexpensive framing materials. The cost of having a number of pictures professionally mounted and framed can be prohibitive, whereas making your own is a satisfying alternative.

In this project we demonstrate how to make a frame measuring approximately 45 x 35 cm (18 x 14 in) overall, with an image size of approximately 30 x 20 cm (12 x 8 in). Obviously, you may construct a frame of almost any size, perhaps to fit a chosen picture or photograph, in which case the measurements must be adjusted accordingly. If you wish, this frame can be made as a mirror rather than a picture frame.

BREAD TIN PLANTER

EQUIPMENT

Medium-grade wire wool
12 mm (½ in) paintbrush
White spirit for brush cleaning

MATERIALS

Metal bread tin
Red oxide primer paint
Spray can of silver paint

METHOD

1 Although the tins had been stacked outdoors, the metallic plating was largely intact, except on the sides where they had been exposed to the weather. Rather than strip and laboriously polish the whole tin, we decided to treat the rust and refinish with silver metal paint. There are a number of silver metal paints currently available, but few accurately simulate a plated finish. The most convincing and effective we found are those produced for the automobile trade, which are available from car accessory shops.

2 Use the medium-grade wire wool to remove the surface rust and reveal a smooth metal substrate. Be careful to work along the length of the tin in order to minimise any unsightly scratching.

3 When you are satisfied with the finish you have achieved, apply one coat of red oxide paint to both the outside and inside of the tin with the paintbrush and leave to dry. Clean the brush with white spirit.

4 Read the manufacturer's directions on the spray paint carefully then, following their instructions, spray one coat of paint on the whole of the exterior of the tin and approximately 25 mm (1 in) down the inside. Be careful not to overspray and cause the paint to drip or sag. Put the tin to one side to dry.

When the paint is dry, the tin can be filled with potting compost and planted. The bread tin has no drainage holes, so plants must be watered from the top. Be careful not to overwater the plants and so cause the potting compost to become waterlogged.

Safety note

Rubber or protective gloves are recommended for this project. Work on a surface protected with newspaper or other disposable covering. Always use spray paints in a dust-free and well-ventilated area, and be careful not to breathe in fumes; we advise you to use a face mask.

Good-looking planters are not always easy to find, but this tin-plated planter filled with pots of pretty flowers or herbs is a wonderful way to smarten up your window sill with a bright, modern look.

The bread tins we found for this project had apparently been made in the 1960s, when industrial action in the baking industry threatened a bread shortage and the nation was being prepared to bake its own bread. Unfortunately, these tins, made by government order, proved too large for the average household oven, and of the thousands made all but a few were scrapped.

DOORSTOP

EQUIPMENT

Handsaw
Electric drill
16 mm (⅝ in) spade or auger drill bit
Hacksaw
Small palette knife
Waxing brush or stiff-bristled paintbrush
Lint-free soft cotton rag

MATERIALS

20 cm (8 in) piece of oak moulding
Two-part epoxy putty (or similar hard-hold
  filler)
Wrought-iron handle
Clear furniture wax

METHOD

1 Trim the end of the oak block to size with the handsaw. Place it on a work surface and drill a hole into the centre to approximately half its depth with the electric drill and spade or auger bit. Remove any sawdust or shavings from the drilled hole.

2 Mix the epoxy putty according to the manufacturer's instructions and place it in the drilled hole. Use the hacksaw to cut the handle shaft to fit the block, then insert it into the filled hole. Remove any excess putty that has been squeezed out with the palette knife. Make sure that the handle is standing upright; put to one side for the putty to set.

   Apply a coat of clear furniture wax to the top, sides and end (but not the bottom) with the waxing brush or stiff-bristled paintbrush and rub it into the wood with the soft cotton rag. When it is dry, polish it with more clean cotton rag.

Unpretentious, this chamfered, golden oak offcut doorstop with a rusty iron door bolt handle, has plenty of rustic charm. The chunky 'green' oak moulded ceiling beam from which it was cut came from the restoration of a seventeenth-century manor house, and the rusty iron door bolt handle was found in our neglected farmhouse kitchen garden. The individual components of the doorstop appear most unpromising, but when assembled the finished doorstop has been much admired. Any number of things can be used to make similar doorstops, and the use of the epoxy putty, which provides a very strong hold, allows numerous different materials to be used. Consider using a nicely rounded stone or large pebble found during a day's beachcombing, with a hole drilled out for the handle, or any pleasing object that has enough weight to hold a door open when spring breezes whip through open windows, blowing the curtains and dislodging the cobwebs.

WINDOW MIRROR

EQUIPMENT

Stiff-bristled paintbrush
Paint stripper
Paint scraper
Wire brush (metal)
Medium-grade glasspaper (wood)
Small stiff brush (an old toothbrush is ideal)
Soft cotton rag
Soft polishing brush
Tape measure
Straight edge
Wax pencil or felt marker (to mark glass)
Glass cutter
Mastic gun (metal)
Light glazing hammer (wood)
Putty knife (wood)
Pliers

MATERIALS

Clear furniture wax
Antique brown furniture wax (wood)
2 mm (1⁄16 in) or 4 mm (3⁄16 in) mirror glass
Brown mastic (metal)
Glazing putty (wood)
Glazing pins (wood)
Screw eyes or fitting lugs (metal)
Heavy-duty picture wire
Pair of mirror plates (wood)

Safety note

Be careful when using paint stripper or working
with glass: most paint strippers are caustic
and glass can splinter when being removed.
Always wear safety goggles and rubber or
protective gloves.

NOTE

For metal-framed windows you need all
the equipment and materials listed except
for those marked '(wood)'. For wooden-
framed windows you need all the
equipment and materials listed except for
those marked '(metal)'.

Windows have been made in a multitude of shapes and sizes and many lend themselves to conversion into stunning ornamental mirrors. Removed when frames have rotted or houses are being 'updated', sometimes an arched or decoratively shaped window can be found without difficulty at an architectural reclamation yard, awaiting transformation into a beautiful mirror.

Before you start working on any frame, give some thought to how you will fix the mirror once completed. Has it somewhere on the reverse where picture wire can be fitted? Does it have holes for screw fixing? Could it be drilled to accept screw eyes or is it worthwhile getting fitting lugs welded to the back? Every window offers a different challenge. If you intend using a wooden frame, can the original fittings be removed without damaging the frame? It is worthwhile thinking through the project before you start. For this project we have selected an ancient cast-iron window saved from a decommissioned church. The window is irregular in shape with no two panes the same size, which adds to the appeal of the mirror and justifies the little extra effort needed to make it.

We have chosen to preserve the aged and pitted appearance of the cast iron on our project mirror, but it could just as easily be painted, gilded or given a distressed finish to add to its romantic appeal.

WINDOW MIRROR

METHOD

Note that alternative methods are given for wooden window frames. Read the instructions thoroughly before you begin to ensure that you use the correct method.

1 Clean the window frame with the stiff-bristled paintbrush then remove all the paint with the paint stripper, being careful to follow the manufacturer's instructions. Paint stripper is caustic so care should be taken. (We suggest using a paint-stripping service, which uses a hot caustic dip system and has the advantage of loosening any glass and putty still present in the frame.) Remove any glass, if you are using a frame with old glass, being careful not to break it, and put to one side. Clean off any residual paint and putty using a paint scraper and wire brush, paying particular attention to the glass rebate. (For wooden frames, use glasspaper instead of a wire brush.)

2 Make sure that the frame is dry and free of any dust or dirt. Apply clear furniture wax to the front of the frame with the small stiff brush, being careful not to get any wax into the glass rebate. Finish with some soft rag. (For wooden frames, wax both front and back, using an antique wax if preferred.) When the wax is dry, polish with the soft brush or soft cotton rag.

3 Carefully measure the glass rebate then mark and cut the mirror glass to the exact size. (If you are wary of cutting glass, a glazier will cut the glass to size for you.) Note that 2 mm (1/16 in) mirror glass is easier to cut than 4 mm (3/16 in) glass and is more suitable for smaller panes. (Because of the small panes in the window selected for this project, we have managed to use mirror glass cut from offcut and waste; we numbered each pane as it was cut to ensure a good fit when assembled.) Using the mastic gun, place a very small bead of mastic inside each frame rebate and fit the mirror glass, pressing it firmly into place. Apply the mastic carefully around the rear of the glass to secure it in place. Repeat until all the panes are filled. (For wooden frames, fill the glass rebate with softened putty and fit the glass in place. Use the glazing hammer and glazing pins to secure the glass. Fill the remaining rebate with putty and finish to a bevelled edge with the putty knife.)

Remove any excess mastic from the mirror surfaces and leave to set. Feed the heavy-duty picture wire through the lugs, screw eyes or plates on the back of the frame and tie in place. Use slip-proof knots and tighten with pliers, tying any excess wire to the lugs. Cast-iron frames are extremely heavy, so make sure that the wire used is sufficiently strong and that the knots used are slip-proof. Caution – when hanging the mirror, ensure that the fixings used will carry the weight of the mirror. Use rawlplugs and screws rather than picture hooks.

TRICK OF THE TRADE

Modern glass is produced by a 'float' process and is free of any blemishes or irregularities; old glass, on the other hand, is often full of imperfections, which can be part of its charm. If you prefer your mirror to have the appearance of antiquity, fit the new mirror glass behind refitted salvaged glass panes or glass cut from an old sheet. Ensure that the window rebate is sufficiently deep to take both sheets of glass and that the old glass and new mirror are clean before you fit them.

The next few pages show a stunning array of shape and form, all united by one thing in common: illumination. Ideas from glamorous, fragile-looking chandeliers to lights made from a

LIGHT AND SHADE

humble roof tile are considered. We take lighting for granted, stretching out an arm to put on a light switch, although even this can now be done by remote control. All it takes, however, is an unexpected power cut to throw us into panic and a frantic search for matches and candles – which usually turn up the moment power is restored!

It seems strange to think that less than fifty years ago many houses, especially in rural areas, had no electricity and that people relied on paraffin lamps and candles to do chores and tasks as well as reading, sewing and other leisure activities. By contrast, today we have so much choice in lighting: unobtrusive low-voltage down-lighters or washes of up-light to accent interior details, and dimmer switches that can swiftly change the mood of a room.

ABOVE

Clear and some coloured plastic knives, forks and spoons have been used to create this eye-catching chandelier. An empty sunflower oil bottle covers the central hanging, while others have been cut down to make the candle cups. Fake candles have been made from the cardboard tubes found inside embroidery wools.

RIGHT

Chandelier by Madeleine Boulesteix, an artist working with a fantastic variety of salvaged materials including toast racks, Pyrex cups, glasses, plug chains and pastry cutters bought at charity shops and car-boot sales.

Lighting should complement the architecture of the area. If a modern chandelier is suspended within a sleek, contemporary interior, the two will blend and harmonise, yet an antique chandelier, sparkling and glowing, hung in the same interior becomes something the eye cannot resist, a dominant design feature and not in the least incongruous.

LEFT

A bulb has been placed under an iron pavement grill, radiating an arc of filtered light on to the wall above in the Bristol restaurant Byzantium.

BOTTOM LEFT

This double Roman terracotta roof tile has been secured to the wall to create an unusual, robust and practical rustic light fitting.

BOTTOM RIGHT

This pillar lamp was designed and made by cabinet maker Richard Wallace from thinly cut and painstakingly joined end grain softwood timber cut from pallets to give a soft, filtered light.

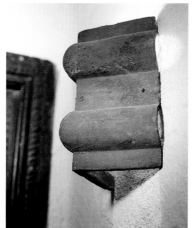

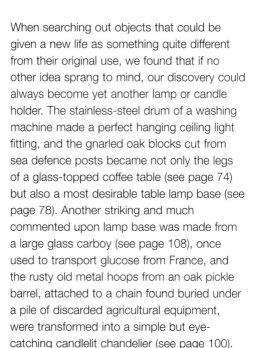

When searching out objects that could be given a new life as something quite different from their original use, we found that if no other idea sprang to mind, our discovery could always become yet another lamp or candle holder. The stainless-steel drum of a washing machine made a perfect hanging ceiling light fitting, and the gnarled oak blocks cut from sea defence posts became not only the legs of a glass-topped coffee table (see page 74) but also a most desirable table lamp base (see page 78). Another striking and much commented upon lamp base was made from a large glass carboy (see page 108), once used to transport glucose from France, and the rusty old metal hoops from an oak pickle barrel, attached to a chain found buried under a pile of discarded agricultural equipment, were transformed into a simple but eye-catching candlelit chandelier (see page 100).

In the chapter 'Wining and Dining', a heavy metal flower display stand bought at auction was recreated as a decorative candle stand (see page 22). Bed springs do not sound too promising, but surmounted with an orb-shaped candle, they can be transformed into a real talking point as a contemporary-looking centrepiece for the table (see page 122). Finally, wooden staircase newel posts, each drilled at one end for a giant candle, become imposing candle holders (see page 126).

HOOP CHANDELIER

EQUIPMENT

Wire brush
Palette knife
Glasspaper
Electric drill and selection of wood bits
Screwdriver
12 mm (½ in) paintbrush
Old toothbrush
Soft polishing brush
Soft cotton rag
Hacksaw

MATERIALS

Two barrel hoops of slightly different
    diameter
Scraps of waste wood
Two-part wood filler
Four mop- or broom-head holders
Eight 18 mm (¾ in) screws
Four 38 mm (1½ in) cup hooks
Four 38 mm (1½ in) screw eyes
Four steel marlin spikes
Four split rings
Four small lanyard hooks
Black satin finish stove paint
Black stove polish
Ceiling hook
Approximately 2.4 m (8 ft) metal chain
Candles

Safety notes

Lit candles are a potential fire hazard, so always
hang your chandelier sufficiently far enough from
the ceiling to ensure that there is no danger of fire
or smoke damage.
Rubber or protective gloves are recommended for
this project.
Make sure that all fittings are secure and that the
chandelier is fastened into a timber ceiling joist or
other structural timber. Under no circumstances
should it be fitted to laths, plaster or plasterboard.

Suspended from the ceiling, this simple but heavy metal design, which evolved from mainly industrial components, is in stark contrast to the delicate appearance of some of our other chandeliers.

As redundant oak whisky barrels or smaller pickle barrels used as garden planters finally give way to rot, remember to salvage the metal hoops. The cooper used these hoops of graduated sizes to secure the shaped wooden lathes in place, and to make this chandelier you will need to select two hoops of slightly different diameters. (Alternatively, you could use a wooden wheel for the frame, or, should you have access to welding equipment, a metal wheel.) You will also need some old-fashioned metal mop-head fixings to make candle holders and a number of heavy steel marlin spikes to dangle underneath. These weighty drops are not merely decorative but help to keep the chandelier both level, compensating for any differences in weight across the frame of the chandelier, and stable to prevent it swinging in inevitable draughts. They could be replaced with any other weighty item that could be attached to the screw eyes. The hoops came from our garden, the mop-head fittings were discovered in a reclamation yard and the steel marlin spikes were sold to us by a rope and sail maker; all the other fittings come from hardware shops. The sturdy chain, absolutely essential to take the weight of the finished chandelier, was part of a lot bought at a farm sale.

HOOP CHANDELIER

METHOD

1 Clean the barrel hoops with a wire brush to remove surface rust and grime. Place them on a work surface, one inside the other, and use scraps of wood to wedge the hoops apart so that a consistent gap is created between the hoops around their circumference. Fill the gap with two-part wood filler (any other plasticised filler that can be drilled and will hold a screw securely is an acceptable alternative) and smooth with the palette knife.

2 Turn the joined hoops over and fill the reverse of the gap with more filler. When the filler has cured, finish with glasspaper. Mark four equally spaced points on one surface of the filled and joined hoops and place a mop-head holder on each. Mark the fixing holes, remove the holders and drill holes to accept the 18 mm (¾ in) fixing screws. Attach the four mop-head holders with screws inserted into the filler.

3 Mark four points on the same side of the joined hoops midway between each fitted mop-head holder, then drill holes for and fit the four cup hooks. Turn the joined hoops over and drill four further holes, this time under the mop-head holders, and fit the screw eyes. (For added strength, the screw eyes and cup hooks can be screwed into the filler before it has fully cured; alternatively, coat their threads with filler before fitting them into the drilled holes.)

4 Paint the cup hooks, screw eyes and mop-head holders, together with the marlin spikes, split rings and lanyard hooks not yet fitted, with black satin finish stove paint and leave to dry. When they are fully dry, take the old toothbrush, dip it into the black stove polish and paint over the chandelier and fittings. When they are dry, polish to a light sheen with the soft brush and cotton rag.

5 Fix the ceiling hook securely to a roof joist or other structural timber above where your chandelier will hang; because of its weight, under no circumstances should it be fitted to laths, plaster or plasterboard. Decide on its height from the ceiling and cut the chain into two lengths, each double that measurement. Place the ends of each chain over opposing cup hooks and the centres on to the ceiling hook in order to hang the chandelier. Fit split rings and lanyard hooks to the marlin spikes and hang them from the screw eyes on the chandelier. Finally, insert candles in the mop-head holders and your chandelier is complete.

HIP TILE CEILING LIGHT

EQUIPMENT

Wire brush
Electric hammer drill
Masonry drill bit
Metal snips
Empty mastic gun
Dry sand or gravel
Metal or strong plastic bucket
Hacksaw
Pliers

MATERIALS

Three clay hip tiles
Waste lead sheet
Lead adhesive
Metal chain
Metal wire
Ceiling hook

SAFETY NOTE

This ceiling light is extremely heavy, so make sure that all fittings are secure and that the ceiling hook is fastened into a timber ceiling joist or other structural timber. Under no circumstances should it be fitted to laths, plaster or plasterboard.

We have always enjoyed the warmth and tradition of terracotta and search for different ways to use and enjoy this natural material.

Weathered roof tiles are particularly attractive, with lichens and water staining adding to their character. Hank Terry of Milo Design used reclaimed tiles as ceiling lights to great effect in the Bristol restaurant Byzantium and he offered to make a light from three hip tiles for this project. Hip tiles are used to cap the joint, or 'hip', of a roof, and innumerable patterns have been produced although all are of much the same general shape.

Terracotta roof tiles used as wall lights are quite a familiar sight in Spain and other Mediterranean countries, and we show you how to make one in the chapter 'Design and Detail' (see page 130).

You may choose to construct your ceiling light with the opening downwards rather than upwards, as ours is made, but whichever way round you choose, the light is heavy and must be hung on a chain fixed to a strong hook driven through the plaster and into a ceiling joist.

Other ideas we have seen for hanging lights are terracotta flower pots hung upside down and suspended from a ceiling, and particularly striking was a seaside villa in Italy where clear wine bottles, in groups of eight or ten, each with a light inside, provided the illumination. Architect Mark Watson has cleverly used a wooden grain hopper to make a shade for a centre light in the high-ceilinged sitting room in his holiday house, which was converted from a former corn mill.

HIP TILE CEILING LIGHT

METHOD

1 Select three hip tiles that are of equal size and relatively undamaged. Using the wire brush, clean off any lichen, dust or dirt from their surface, paying particular attention to the inside (or concave) surfaces. With the electric drill and masonry bit, drill a hole in the centre of the splayed end of each tile. Drill from the outside (or convex) side to prevent unsightly flaking of the clay surface where the drill bit emerges.

2 Cut the waste lead sheet with the metal snips into three strips each approximately 10 cm (4 in) wide and the length of the tiles. Place two tiles together, concave side up and supported by wooden blocks or spare tiles so that the edges fit tightly together and, using a mastic gun, apply a liberal quantity of lead adhesive to the full length of both tiles, approximately 50 mm (2 in) from both sides of the join. Press one cut lead strip on to the adhesive and press down to make a secure joint.

3 Place a quantity of dry sand or gravel into the bucket to support the tiles, then gently place the joined tiles into the bucket, pointed end down, and place the third tile in the bucket to make a tightly fitting cone shape of three tiles. It may prove necessary to add or remove sand or gravel to support the tiles properly in the bucket. When you are satisfied with the construction, apply lead adhesive approximately 50 mm (2 in) from both sides of the two remaining joins and secure with the lead strips. Make sure that the lead strips are securely bonded to the adhesive, then leave for at least twenty-four hours or until the adhesive has cured.

Remove the tiles from the bucket and clean off any residual adhesive. Measure three lengths of chain to slightly more than the height at which you wish to hang the finished light from the ceiling and cut to length with the hacksaw. Fit the chain lengths to the drilled holes in the tiles with metal wire and secure with the pliers. Use the pliers to make sure that the chain is securely fitted. Hang the finished light from the chains fitted to a hook driven into the ceiling.

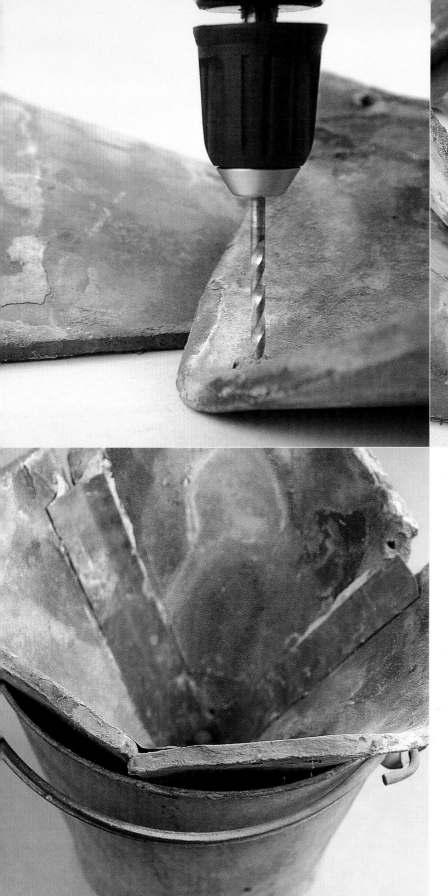

CARBOY LAMP

EQUIPMENT

Electric drill
32 mm (1¼ in) tank cutting bit (to fit inside
    the bottle top)
Glasspaper
Multi-speed electrical tool and sanding
    head (optional)
18 mm (¾ in) auger or spade drill bit
Round wood file
Wood filler or two-part filling compound
    (optional)
Hammer
Glass cleaner
Lint-free cotton rag or absorbent kitchen
    paper
Electrician's screwdriver

MATERIALS

Piece of 50 mm (2 in) thick wood (preferably
    softwood)
Glass carboy bottle
Bottle lamp holder with side fitting and
    adjustable stem and lamp cord attached
Lamp holder
Lampshade
60 watt electric light bulb
Fused electric plug

METHOD

1 Use the 32 mm (1¼ in) tank cutting bit to cut a plug out of the piece of 50 mm (2 in) thick timber. You will have to measure the diameter of the inside of the top of the bottle you are using and cut a plug slightly larger than that measurement. Use glasspaper or the multi-speed electrical tool and sanding head to sand the plug down to a lightly tapered shape until it will fit tightly inside the top of the bottle.

2 Use the electric drill and auger or spade bit, placed in the hole already cut in the centre of the plug, to cut a second hole, 18 mm (¾ in) in diameter, in the plug. Again, this measurement depends on the bottle lamp holder you are using. Most are made from plastic and the stem is designed to compress to fit differing hole sizes, so adjust the size of your hole to fit. If necessary, enlarge this hole to fit the lamp holder stem with the round wood file or multi-speed electrical tool and sanding head.

3 Gently insert the stem of the lamp holder inside the plug so that it is securely held. If the lamp holder is loose, you can use wood filler or two-part filling compound to fix it in place.

Clean the inside of the bottle, because once the lamp holder is inserted you will not be able to clean it. A simple way to remove staining from the inside of a glass container is to fill it with a small amount of sharp gravel and shake vigorously. Rinse with hot soapy water and leave to drain.

4 Carefully place the wooden plug and lamp holder into the top of the bottle; it should be a tight fit. Tap the plug home into the bottle using a hammer cushioned with a scrap of timber, gently working around the circumference of the plug. If the plug is too tight a fit, there is a danger that you may break the bottle as the plug is driven home, so err on the side of caution, remove the plug and lamp holder, sand off a little more wood and try again until the plug sits securely inside the neck of the bottle.

Clean the outside of the bottle with glass cleaner and polish with cotton rag or absorbent kitchen paper. Unscrew the top of the lamp holder and fit the shade holder and your chosen lampshade. Insert the light bulb and attach the fused electric plug to the lamp cord fitted to the lamp holder.

Safety note

Electricity can be dangerous; if you are in any doubt, we advise that all electrical fittings are checked by a qualified electrician. If a metal lamp holder is used, it is vital that three-core wire is used and that the earth is connected to both the lamp holder and the electric plug.

Hand-blown glass has an enduring appeal. It is strong and fluid yet fragile and delicate, with light dancing off to reflect its shape and the colours of the room around. The carboy we selected as a lamp base is a utilitarian clear glass bottle that was originally designed to transport large quantities of glucose from France for use in the English wine-making trade, protected by a wooden cradle in transit. Since glass resists corrosion, carboys were also used to transport acid, but these bottles have now been replaced by plastic to ensure that the contents last the journey. No two carboys are identical, differing slightly in the overall shape, the bubbles embedded in the glass and in colour – they can sometimes be found in a glorious green hue.

Some of the bottles filled with brightly coloured liquids that at one time were seen in every chemist's window would, if one could buy them, convert into superb lamps and, since fashion is cyclical, we may again see Chianti bottles in their woven grass cradles converted into lamps, just as they once were seen in every self-respecting bistro throughout the 1960s.

GLOBE LIGHT

EQUIPMENT

Electric drill
12 mm (½ in) auger or spade drill bit
Tenon saw
High-speed multi-purpose tool with saw
    attachment (optional)
12 mm (½ in) wood chisel
Lint-free cotton rag
Electrician's screwdriver

MATERIALS

Wooden tent pole base plate (or similar
    wooden round)
Medium brown furniture wax
18 mm (¾ in) screws
Brown frame sealant
Green baize or felt
Rubberised glue
Glass globe

ELECTRICAL

Approx. 2 m (2 yd) two-core electrical amp
    flex (or three-core if a metal lamp fitting
    is used)
Metal or plastic flat-based lamp holder
Fused electric plug
Electric light bulb (60 watt maximum)

METHOD

1 Take the tent pole base plate and drill through the centre from the top with the 12 mm (½ in) auger or spade bit. It is advisable to place the base plate on a piece of waste wood, unless your work surface will not mind the drill bit passing into it. (If you are using a wooden round with no indented area, you must drill or cut a rebate in the top sufficient to house the globe glass light comfortably.)

2 Turn the wooden base over so that the bottom faces upwards and, with a tenon saw, make two cuts approximately 12 mm (½ in) apart and 12 mm (½ in) deep leading from the drilled centre hole to the outside edge. (A high-speed multi-purpose tool with saw attachment will make very short work of this job.) Use the 12 mm (½ in) wood chisel to remove the wood between the saw cuts to leave a groove for the electric lamp flex.

3 Apply a liberal application of medium brown furniture wax to the top and sides of the base, rubbing it well into the wood with clean, lint-free cotton rag. Make sure not to get any wax on the bottom surface of the base. Leave the wax to dry and be absorbed into the wood, then polish with some more clean rag. A second application of wax will improve the finish.

4 Pass the electric lamp flex up through the centre of the wooden base and, with the electrician's screwdriver, fit it to the flat-based lamp holder. Screw the lamp holder to the bottom of the rebate in the base with the 18 mm (¾ in) screws. Fit the electric plug to the other end, pull the flex taught and secure into the groove cut in the bottom of the base with brown frame sealant. Leave the sealant to cure.

When the sealant has cured, cut the baize or felt to the shape of the bottom of the lamp base and fit in place with rubberised glue. When the glue has dried, insert an electric light bulb into the lamp holder and place the glass globe light over the top.

Safety note

Electricity can be dangerous; if you are in any doubt, we advise that all electrical fittings are checked by a qualified electrician. If a metal lamp holder is used, it is vital that three-core wire is used and that the earth wire is connected to both the lamp holder and the electric plug.

To make this simple but effective light, with its soft, unobtrusive glow, you need only three main components: a base, a shade and the electrical fittings.

In our constant search for salvaged materials, we often turn to the detritus-filled premises of our friendly government surplus supplier. We knew from experience that after a couple of hours in his premises we would leave full of inspiration and, fortunately for him, several purchases. Clambering into the back of a malodorous old container body used as storage in the yard we hit upon rows of wooden rounds, which resembled truckles of farmhouse cheeses lined up in a dairy.

We were unable to guess their origins, but Lawrence enlightened us: they were the turned ash or beech pole base plates used to stop the poles of old marquees sinking into soft ground. After many years of service, the canvas marquees became redundant. They were then either passed on to the Boy Scouts or donated to charities, who send them out as emergency relief shelters to disaster areas worldwide (minus their wooden feet). Marquees in too poor a state of repair for use were burnt or thrown away, and all that was left behind were the tent poles, pole bases and guy rope pegs we discovered on our visit.

The spherical glass, opalescent, clear or sometimes patterned, can be found in different sizes from architectural reclamation yards. We found ours at Au Temps Perdu, where owner John Chapman, an enthusiast and mine of information, told us that they were the enclosed covers for bathroom lights.

COLUMN LAMP

The column lamp we have featured here was designed by John Edmonds. The vertical beam of light thrown by the hole in the top of the column and the muted illumination shining through the wooden beading and tissue paper used in its construction give this light an Eastern feel.

John has designed a number of lamps using everything from lead, old terracotta land drains rescued after almost two hundred years underground, figured and ancient oak and elm, and even glass salvaged from the cockpit of a dismantled aircraft. He has been working with recycled materials for thirty years and now employs over twenty designers and craftsmen working in timber, stone, metal and glass, interpreting his designs, making and restoring furniture and undertaking a variety of design, construction and restoration projects throughout Britain and abroad.

The column lamp can be made in various sizes, from hardwood, softwood or any number of different materials. For this project we have selected timber cut from old softwood joists for the base and column construction and salvaged beading for the connecting structure. Redundant brass stair rods also make unusual connectors.

EQUIPMENT

Electric planer or hand plane
Try square
Sash clamps
Medium-grade glasspaper
Sanding block
Tape measure
Compass made from string, pencil and
	drawing pin
Jigsaw and fine wood-cutting blade
Electric drill
12 mm (½ in) spade drill bit
Straight edge
Handsaw
Soft cotton rag
Hammer
12 mm (½ in) wood chisel or craft knife
Waxing brush or stiff-bristled paintbrush
Paste brush
Electrician's screwdriver

MATERIALS

The project lamp has been designed as a table lamp but all dimensions are approximate and can be adjusted for the materials available and the size of the lamp you are making, which may be scaled up or down.

Approx. 2 m (2 yd) of 20 cm x 50 mm (8 x 2
	in) salvaged softwood joists
Wood glue
Furniture wax polish
Approx. 9 m (9 yd) of 18 x 10 mm (¾ x ⅜ in)
	planed quadrant, cut into twelve 75 cm
	(30 in) lengths
Tissue or other translucent paper
	(handmade paper is an alternative)
Wallpaper paste

ELECTRICAL

Fused electric plug
Two-core lamp flex (or three-core if a metal
	lamp fitting is used)
Plastic batten lamp holder
Electric light bulb (60 watt maximum)

Safety note

Electricity can be dangerous; if you are in any doubt, we advise that all electrical fittings are checked by a qualified electrician. If metal lamp fittings are used, it is vital that three-core wire is used and that the earth wire is connected to both the lamp holder and the electric plug.

COLUMN LAMP

METHOD

1 Cut the 20 cm x 5 mm (8 x 2 in) softwood joists into four 30 cm (12 in) lengths and two 38 cm (15 in) lengths. Plane one edge of each cut length, making sure that it is square with the try square. Take two pieces of each cut length and, using glue and sash clamps, join them together planed edge to planed edge. Repeat with the remaining lengths until you have two pieces of timber 40 x 30 cm (16 x 12 in) and one 40 x 38 cm (16 x 15 in). Leave for at least twenty-four hours to dry before removing the sash clamps. When the glue is dry, plane the faces of the timber and use the glasspaper and sanding block to finish.

Mark a point at the centre of face of the 38 cm (15 in) joined length. Take a length of string and tie one end to a drawing pin placed firmly on the centre mark and tie a pencil to the other end of the string, 18 cm (7 in) from the centre, to make a simple compass. Holding the centre pin in one hand and the pencil in the other, draw a 36 cm (14 in) circle on the board to create the outline of the lamp base; put to one side. Shorten the string to 14 cm (5½ in) and draw circles 28 cm (11 in) in diameter on both 30 cm (12 in) joined lengths to create outlines for the column base and top. Shorten the string to 75 mm (3 in) and, using the same centre points, draw two further circles, 15 cm (6 in) in diameter, inside the 28 cm (11 in) drawn circles.

2 Using the jigsaw, cut carefully round the rings to make three circular boards, one 36 cm (14 in) and two 28 cm (11 in) in diameter. Cut 12 mm (½ in) holes in the centres of all three boards with the electric drill and spade bit. Take the 36 cm (14 in) board (lamp base) and, on the underside starting at the drilled centre hole, draw two lines 12 mm (½ in) apart with a pencil to the outside edge. Use the handsaw to cut along the pencil lines to a depth of approximately 10 mm (⅜ in), then remove the waste wood with the wood chisel to create a channel for the lamp flex. Cut out 15 cm (6 in) centres in the 28 cm (11 in) column base and top, using the drilled hole for jigsaw blade access. Smooth the exposed sawn edges with glasspaper.

3 Depending on the final appearance desired, wax and polish the column base and top and lamp base with the soft rag to the desired finish. Take the column base and top and, with the drill and spade bit, cut twelve equally spaced holes around the outside of both boards approximately 18 mm (¾ in) from the outside edge and approximately 12 mm (½ in) deep. Ensure that the twelve 75 cm (30 in) lengths of quadrant beading are free from knots or bends and trim the ends with a chisel or craft knife to fit tightly into 12 mm (½ in) holes. Drive the twelve sections of beading into the drilled holes to join the column base and top, and secure with wood glue. Leave to dry.

4 Take a number of approximately 1 m (1 yd) torn lengths of your selected paper, paste one side with wallpaper paste, then carefully stretch them round the lamp over the beading. When the beading is covered to your satisfaction (several layers may be required), leave the paper to dry. You have now completed the construction of your lamp.

Fit the fused plug to one end of the electric lamp flex. Feed the other end of the flex from the underside of the lamp base through the drilled hole and fit it to the plastic batten lamp holder, screwed to the top of the base over the hole. Place the light bulb in the lamp holder then place the assembled column over the top.

In this chapter we illustrate a number of designs that are firstly functional but must work visually too. It is worth remembering that even when a design has been specially commissioned, it can

Where companies or individuals have conscientiously striven to salvage and reuse materials, the end results can be superb. Handmade clay bricks have a wonderful depth of colour,

DESIGN AND DETAIL

be quite a challenge to make it work in a practical sense, and when the item or product is old and has been made for another entirely different use or situation, the challenge is that much greater. Of course, the easy way out is to buy 'off the shelf', rather than consider how something might be adapted for reuse, but finding a solution is half the fun!

and even the heavy bricks rescued from the inside of outdated night store heaters, which usually end their days as hard core, make stunning floors. Roof slates, laid on concrete, their nail holes filled with lead and polished to a gleam, can be transfigured into a floor of great beauty that seems to stretch to infinity.

TOP 1

Solid mahogany doors, rescued from a redundant bank, divide the entrance hall in this house from a more formal inner hall. The gold leaf lettering is original.

TOP 2

Wooden staircase spindles have been cut down the middle lengthways to provide a decorative detail for the shelves of a well-proportioned but plain bookcase at Charlton House Hotel.

TOP 3

Milo Design have used roof slates salvaged from a church to cover a large floor area in the Bristol restaurant Byzantium.

TOP 4

Once installed in an ancient manor house, this floor was taken up at some stage and subsequently found piled into buckets in a reclamation yard. Although badly damaged, it was reassembled and relaid, with any missing sections cleverly matched up.

TOP 5

This well-worn but delicately patterned early encaustic terracotta floor once belonged in a historic and rather grand Jacobean house.

TOP 6

This oak staircase was designed by architect Mark Watson for a converted stable block, with a curved oak stall partition forming the handrail. The iron supports and elm boards on the wall behind were reclaimed from the original building.

RIGHT

This balcony was built in the converted barn adjoining designer John Edmonds' farmhouse to divide a bedroom from the seating area below. The supports were made from driftwood, dried and air blasted with crushed walnut shells, and the rail and base from aged oak faced with spalted (diseased) elm.

Wood for floors is probably the most commonly reclaimed and reused material. Medieval oak cut from French farm buildings, pitch pine planks cut from a Victorian mill, a parquet floor in some exotic hardwood rescued from a modest office building, or yellow pine from a redundant factory all cry out for rescue and sympathetic treatment. Most striking of all was an interlocking gymnasium floor taken up, its original markings preserved and relaid in an apparently random pattern – seemingly simple but a time-consuming task. Where time and money are involved, it is easy to see why so many good-quality materials are dumped or destroyed by contractors anxious to complete their work within a deadline.

It's all in the detail. Detail is the molten lead that filled the nail holes in a slated floor or the simplicity of a moulded block of wood used to hold open a door; the care the craftsman takes to carve the finest shape; the incongruous choice of colour in a casually placed object. All those things that

accentuate, add interest and make a room complete make such an important contribution to the overall design.

Ornamental and decorative detail is shown in the unknown origins of the textured leather moulding in the entrance hall or the split wooden staircase spindle, which added another dimension to an otherwise ordinary bookcase at Charlton House Hotel; the gold leaf lettering on a mahogany door in a Wiltshire house and the distinctive walnut shell blasted driftwood balcony in John Edmonds' home. All have a beauty, fascinating, functionless but exquisite in their shapes and hues.

Not all detail needs be purely decorative. An original, basic but functional wooden lock on a sixteenth-century oak door, and plain metal rods that perfectly complement a reclaimed oak staircase rescued from the same building are practical features but at the same time they help to break up a line and relieve the eye from too much timber – pure and simple, and yet precise.

SPINDLE BOOKCASE

EQUIPMENT

Pliers
Bench saw or band saw
Tenon saw
Hammer
18 mm (¾ in) wood chisel
Craft knife (optional)
Glasspaper
Electric drill
Drill bit to fit 75 mm (3 in) screws
Screwdriver
Waxing brush or stiff-bristled paintbrush
Soft lint-free cotton rag
Soft polishing brush

MATERIALS

Several stair spindles
Old bookcase
45 mm (1¾ in) panel pins
Wood glue
Four bun feet
Four 75 mm (3 in) screws
Antique brown furniture wax

METHOD

1 Before commencing the construction of this bookcase, the spindles must be split in half along their length. It is perfectly possible, if extremely time-consuming, to do this with a handsaw, but a much better result can be achieved if the spindles are cut with a bench or band saw. Remember before you start cutting to remove any nails that may still be present in the spindles; failure to do this may result in serious damage to the machinery and, more importantly, may cause the spindle being cut to 'snatch', resulting in injury to the machine operator.

2 Lay the bookcase on its back on a work surface, select two half-spindles for the sides of the bookcase, trim them to size with the tenon saw and secure temporarily in place with panel pins. For the shelves, we have used spindles cut so that two opposing pieces cut from the one spindle make a balanced pattern on each shelf. Should you wish to achieve a more idiosyncratic appearance, use one whole cut spindle for each shelf front. Shape the ends where they butt against the spindles attached to the bookcase sides with a chisel or craft knife and glasspaper to make a tight fit. Secure temporarily with panel pins.

3 Remove all the temporarily fitted spindles, apply wood glue to them and replace with the panel pins driven well home. If your bookcase is not fitted with feet, the spindle fitted to the bottom shelf may prevent it standing properly. It is simple to add feet to raise it slightly off the floor to eliminate this problem. We have used softwood bun feet made from cut-down old tent pole finials. Drill though each foot from the underside, apply wood glue and secure to the bottom corners of the bookcase with 75 mm (3 in) screws.

4 Put the bookcase on one side to allow the glue to dry thoroughly. When it is dry, apply antique brown furniture wax with a waxing brush or stiff-bristled paintbrush, paying particular attention to ensuring that the wax is brushed into the corners and the spindle mouldings. Rub the wax well into the wood with the soft cotton rag, and leave to dry. Polish with the soft polishing brush and finish with clean cotton rag. A greater density of colour can be achieved with a second application of wax, and the finish can be maintained by occasional polishing with a soft cloth.

Safety note

If you are using any power-cutting equipment, particularly a bench or band saw, eye protection should be used. We advise that protective gloves are used for this project.

Spindles are the turned supports for the banister rail on a staircase. Made in many different lengths, they were made in their millions when wood-turning machinery was introduced. They are easy to find and here we suggest some uses for them. Matching or not, barley twist or plain, spindles split in half make a decorative and inexpensive moulding perfectly suited to enhance a modest shelf unit to give it a presence it might otherwise not have. Split spindles can adorn all sorts of other furniture, from kitchen cupboards and bathroom units to wooden mirrors, and in this chapter we also show you how to turn one into an elegant candlestick.

You could undertake this project leaving both the bookcase and spindles in their original painted state. However, if you wish to do this, all paintwork should be cleaned with sugar soap, rubbed down with glasspaper and undercoated before being repainted. Old bookcases and spindles often have several layers of paint, and the thickness of these coats can obscure some of the finer and more attractive detail. We recommend that to achieve the best results the bookcase and spindles should be stripped.

Stripping can be undertaken using a commercially available paint stripper, but this is a laborious and unpleasant job that requires protective gloves and clothing. Much more simple is to have your bookcase and spindles stripped by one of the numerous professional stripping services, which use a hot caustic bath to achieve an excellent result.

BED SPRING CANDLE HOLDERS

EQUIPMENT

Fine-grade wire wool
Metal polish
Soft cotton rag

MATERIALS

Bed spring
Metal lacquer spray
Globe-shaped candle

METHOD

1 Gently remove any corrosion with the wire wool, taking care not to rub off the copper plating. Apply the metal polish with a soft cotton rag and burnish with a clean rag. Spray with metal lacquer to preserve the finish and prevent subsequent tarnishing. Place a globe-shaped candle in the top of each spring.

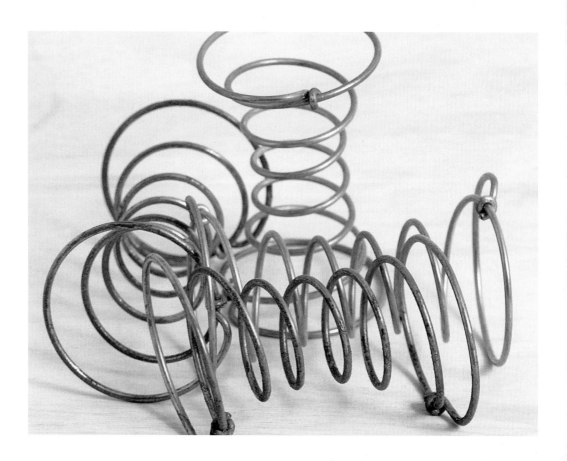

They may compare unfavourably to a pair of solid silver candlesticks passed down through the family over several generations, but our bed spring candle holders are certain to become a talking point, if not a conversation stopper. They illustrate the point that the most unlikely objects can be turned into something desirable and these coiled candle holders are both unusual and, more importantly, fun. Like many people, we have collected candlesticks in many different sizes and materials, from ceramics, glass and metal to a set of five we designed and had turned by a local craftsman from fallen, diseased sycamore, graduating in size from over 1.5 m (48 in) to less than 30 cm (12 in) in height.

We have candles in Victorian ink bottles, night lights in dimpled glasses found at car boot sales, and others in small terracotta flower pots that we have covered with gilt and silver leaf to make a festive table display, particularly at Christmas. As long as the candle fits safely into its receptacle and does not overbalance, there is no limit to the number of objects that can be adapted to become candle holders. Flickering candlelight can illuminate every room of your home!

Scrap yards and car-breakers are good hunting grounds, and at one we managed to salvage a number of copper-plated steel bed or chair springs with the plating still intact. The coiled, almost sculptural shape of these springs, surmounted by globe-shaped candles, suggests that they may have been commissioned by a master metal-smith.

WOOD BLOCK TABLE

EQUIPMENT

Tape measure
Large set square
Chalk or felt-tip pen
Chain saw
Sanding flap disc
Angle grinder
Fibre sanding disc

MATERIALS

Large wooden block or post

METHOD

1 Measure the block and calculate how it can be cut into two equal parts, both having ends that are square. Translate these measurements on to the wooden block using the set square and chalk or felt-tip pen. Prop the block on scrap wood so that is raised off the ground and, being careful to follow the chalk or ink marks, cut off one end square with the chain saw. Continue with the chain saw until you have two equally sized blocks and are satisfied that the ends are square.

2 Fit the sanding flap disc to the angle grinder and remove any rough, discoloured or damaged timber from the sides and one end; work slowly along the length of the block to minimise unsightly sanding marks. Finish to a smooth surface with the angle grinder and fibre sanding disc.

The finished blocks, complete with the evidence of chain sawing on their exposed tops, make extremely effective occasional or lamp tables, perfect for a minimalist interior.

Safety note

Chain saws are potentially extremely dangerous. If you are unfamiliar with their use, seek professional help.
In any event, always use a powerbreaker plug and wear full protective clothing and eye protection when using a chain saw. Eye protection and a dust mask should also be used when sanding with an angle grinder.

Unlikely as it may seem, these unusually large chunks of timber, which weigh enough to make you regret not weight training before you move them, once supported the metal crash barriers between opposing lanes on a motorway. Now that they are slowly being replaced by purpose-made metal supports, we were able to acquire enough for our needs.

Not wishing to compromise the masculine shape and powerful form of the supports, we felt that the best option was to make them slightly more manageable by cutting them in half to make two smaller cubes. With the warmth of the honey gold wood, they are beautiful in their simplicity, works of art, set off with a ceramic pot and placed either side of our Railway Bed (see page 40).

Should you have difficulty in locating a similar motorway barrier block, any large wooden block will serve just as well, and the project is ideally suited to an old tree trunk or bole, squared off to size.

SPINDLE CANDLESTICK

EQUIPMENT

Hammer
Glasspaper
Tape measure
Electric drill
25 mm (1 in) spade drill bit
Pliers
Tenon saw
Set square
38 mm (1½ in) wood chisel
Craft knife
Sash or G clamp

MATERIALS

18 cm (7 in) square of 12 mm (½ in) thick
    plywood or medium density fibreboard
    (MDF)
18 cm (7 in) square of 25 mm (1 in) thick
    softwood plank
Wood glue
32 mm (1¼ in) panel pins
Stair spindle

This elegant candlestick was made from a turned wooden spindle. Found in differing lengths and designs in most reclamation yards, spindles are commonly made of softwood, although as many were made from species of wood no longer harvested, some can be quite hard.

Because so many spindles were made but there are not all that many uses for them, many yards end up burning them for firewood. Spindles are very often varnished or painted when acquired but can be professionally stripped in a bath of hot caustic soda or stripped by hand with commercial paint stripper, as we did to the spindle used for this project. Time-consuming and unpleasant though it is, the result is well worth the effort and we achieved the bleached, aged effect we sought.

Stripped spindles can be waxed and polished, or left unstripped and repainted if preferred, although they should be rubbed down and undercoated before a new coat of paint is applied. We chose to leave the spindle unpolished and selected the 18 cm (7 in) square piece of 25 mm (1 in) softwood plank to match it for colour and texture. Whichever way you treat your spindle, there is great pleasure to be derived from the soft, warm glow of candlelight. You may choose to make any length of candlestick from old spindles, the size being dependent only on the length of the spindle used. Some spindle patterns have square mouldings along their length and these can be used to create shorter candlesticks.

SPINDLE CANDLESTICK

METHOD

1 Join the squares of plywood and softwood together with wood glue and hammer together with 32 mm (1¼ in) panel pins. Plywood or MDF glued to the softwood will prevent it distorting and ensure that the candlestick has a flat base for stability. Use the glasspaper to smooth off the sawn edges.

2 When the glue has dried, mark the centre of the softwood square, place the base on a piece of waste timber and, with the electric drill and 25 mm (1 in) spade bit, drill a hole though both the softwood and the plywood underneath. For a neat finish, drill until the tip of the bit emerges, then turn over and complete the hole, drilling from the plywood side.

3 Take the spindle, use the pliers to remove any nails, then trim both ends square with the tenon saw. Select which end of the spindle is to be the top and which is to be inserted into the base. (This will usually be evident: the end with the shorter section of square moulding will form the top.) Sand off the sawn edges on the top end.

4 Draw a line with a pencil and the set square round the bottom of the spindle 38 mm (1½ in) from the end. Use the tenon saw to make a cut on each face to leave about 25 mm (1 in) uncut wood at the centre. Prise off the cut wood with the wood chisel to leave a core of approximately 25 mm (1 in) in the end. Trim to the exact measurement with the craft knife and glasspaper.

5 Turn the spindle round so that you are able to work on the top and clamp it to the work surface with a sash or G clamp to hold it securely in place. Mark the centre at the top of the end of the spindle with a pencil and carefully drill a hole approximately 18 mm (¾ in) deep with the electric drill and spade bit.

6 Apply wood glue to the trimmed 25 mm (1 in) end of the spindle and insert it into the previously drilled 25 mm (1 in) hole made in the base. Trim off any wood that protrudes below the bottom of the base, ensure that the inserted spindle is vertical, then wipe off any residual wood glue and leave to set.

HIP TILE WALL LIGHT

EQUIPMENT

Wire brush
Battery-powered electric drill
Masonry drill bit
Electrician's screwdriver

MATERIALS

Clay roof hip tile
Angled batten lamp holder
Five rawlplugs
Two 38 mm (1½ in) screws
Electric light bulb (60 watt maximum)
Three 65 mm (2½ in) screws

METHOD

1 Select a hip tile with a curve such that when placed on a flat surface it is sufficiently deep to house the angled batten lamp holder and electric light bulb easily. Place it on the work surface and remove any residual cement, lichen or unsightly staining with the wire brush. With the concave side down, drill three holes with the electric drill and masonry bit, one at the centre of the apex and one at each of the bottom corners. It is a good idea to drill through the tile into a piece of scrap timber; drill carefully and try to prevent the tile being damaged by the emerging drill bit. When the tile is drilled, put it to one side.

2 Make sure that the power is turned off at the mains. Hold the angled batten lamp holder over the wires emerging from the wall in the location you wish to fix it, mark the screw holes with a pencil and put it to one side. Use the battery-operated electric drill and masonry bit to drill holes to a depth of approximately 38 mm (1½ in) at the points marked with a pencil; insert a rawlplug in each. Be careful not to drill into concealed wires. Fit the wires emerging from the wall securely to the reverse of the angled batten

lamp holder, then fix the lamp holder itself to the wall with the 38 mm (1½ in) screws driven into the rawlplugs.

3 Fit the light bulb to the lamp holder and place the hip tile carefully over it in the position desired. For a down-lighter, the opening should face down; for an up-lighter, the opening should face up. Mark the holes drilled in the tile with a pencil and put it to one side. Drill holes at least 50 mm (2 in) deep at the three marked points, being very careful not to drill through concealed electric wires, and insert the rawlplugs. Replace the hip tile in position and secure to the wall using the 65 mm (2½ in) screws driven into the rawlplugs.

Clay hip tiles are extremely heavy, so make sure that the finished light is securely fitted to the wall and that fixings are sufficiently strong to take the weight. For safety, make sure that the light bulb does not touch either the wall or the rear of the tile. When you are satisfied with the appearance of your wall light, switch on the power.

Safety note

Electricity is dangerous; we advise that a properly qualified and experienced electrician is consulted before any electrical work is undertaken. Always turn off the electricity at the mains before starting any work. When drilling close to a fitted wall light, be very careful not to damage buried wires.

A good investment is a wire detector, which can be used to locate hidden electrical cables, thus minimising the danger of damaging wiring when drilling.

Wall lights can add a quality of light and ambience to a room quite impossible to achieve with ceiling lights, however decorative they are. The variety of wall lights that can be bought from interior design and lighting shops is extensive, but many salvaged materials can be used to make quite singular and attractive alternatives.

Old car headlamps can be adapted to serve as effective wall lights, just as other car parts, including the hubcaps fitted to wire holders, can be converted into stunning shaded wall lights. The everyday metal kitchen colander cries out to be a wall light; in fact, there is no reason why you should not be able to make a wall light out of almost anything that takes your fancy.

We have selected hip tiles for this project because they are readily found, inexpensive to buy and come in numerous different shapes, patterns and sizes. Hank and Sophia Terry of Milo Design have used a number of different hip, ridge and roofing tiles in numerous innovative interiors, and examples of some of these are illustrated elsewhere in this book.

Finally, hip tiles can be used as both up-lighters, with the opening at the top, or turned over, as we demonstrate in this project, to act as down-lighters to illuminate a painting or a piece of furniture, or to provide muted atmospheric and unusual lighting.

When the sun shines, the birds sing and the flora is sweetly fragrant, it is time to retreat to the garden inviting family and friends to join in long, lazy lunches that last the whole afternoon or cast-iron sewing machine base to form one of those tables so popular in cafés and pub gardens; or even convert huge wooden cable drums into tables.

Alternatively, why not create an

SEATING AND RETREATING

romantic, moonlit supper parties that finish well into the night.

Create a romantic arbour using telegraph poles as supports in a shaded, secret area, somewhere to eat not too far from the house, and build a barbecue of bricks reclaimed from a storage heater.

As the focal point of the dining area, you could construct a table from enormous stones or boulders topped with a slab of slate or flagstone; rejuvenate a sturdy old wooden table by giving it a metal top; adapt a eye-catching garden feature by making a mosaic-covered table out of shells collected when combing the beach or broken tiles and china unearthed while digging the garden? We show old wooden cheese presses placed on top of slender tree trunks which have a certain rustic charm. In complete contrast, a concrete slab, once the side of a coal bunker but now a table surface on a base of built-up breeze blocks, has more the look of semi-industrial chic!

NEAR RIGHT

An abandoned old blue lias stone flagstone has been installed to make a charming garden seat beneath an arch covered in clematis.

CENTRE LEFT

Glorious garden playhouse beautifully proportioned and made of salvaged corrugated iron with cut tin embellishments, erected in a city garden.

CENTRE RIGHT

'The Seat of Conversion' made by sculptor Paul Grellier from a rescued wayside cross and a variety of salvaged metal and wooden components.

FAR RIGHT

The miniature 'Little House' in the grounds of Nigel and Rosalie Dawes' thirteenth-century moated manor house, Birtsmorton Court. Built of reclaimed timber at Ronsons Reclamation by David Jones, Nigel had it re-erected in the grounds of his medieval house, now open as a corporate hospitality centre.

ABOVE

Detail of a garden seat 'In Suspension' by sculptor Paul Grellier, showing some of the character and colouration of corroded ancient iron and weathered elm timber.

LEFT

This quiet patio area sitting high up on a slope and overlooking the garden has been floored with old clay roofing tiles retained behind a railway sleeper.

Different areas of a garden, or rooms, should have different feels. Strategically placed seating provides places to retreat to according to one's mood and adds character to a garden. Make unusual garden seats from sections of cast-iron grills salvaged from an old greenhouse. Use old scaffold boards or pallets or even timber salvaged from trees blown over in the gales to make benches, swing seats, or oversized bench/tables. Seats can be cut from the stump of an old tree. Saw up old wooden ladders no longer considered safe to make authentic ladderback chairs. Cut in half old oak whisky barrels for tub seats or take a disused dining chair and plant the seat with camomile or your favourite herb. Furnish a sunny arbour with a pine chapel bench. Someone even thought to make a seat out of an old cast-iron bath cut in half! Why not make yourself comfortable in the garden shed and make a wooden bench on which to perch when busy at the potting stand?

Visit historic houses and gardens in order to see for yourself fine architectural gems and gain ideas. You might be inspired to design and build a folly or temple from period salvage, using old floorboards, doors, windows and shutters to create a glorious hideaway, installing a wood-burning stove for warmth. If building is beyond your budget, let loose your imagination and transform an old tool shed, privy or henhouse, giving yourself somewhere to sit quietly and contemplate. Inspired by nature make a den, shelter or a simple retreat.

Inspired by the Romans, grottos were a feature of many landscaped gardens of the eighteenth century and these in turn might inspire you to create a grotto of your own, whatever the size of your garden, a magical space decorated with beautiful shells, planted with shade-loving, large-leafed plants, with the sound of trickling water to add to the atmosphere. The Lost Gardens of Heligan, in Cornwall, houses a grotto lined with rock crystal which reflects candlelight beautifully, adding to its drama. In stark contrast, a mysterious cave we know is lined with prehistoric animal bones, just to put a shiver down the spine!

SCAFFOLD BENCH

EQUIPMENT

Paintbrush
Tape measure
Try-square
Pencil or marker pen
Hand saw
Hammer
Wood chisel
Electric (or hand) screwdriver
Electric (or hand) drill
Selection wood drill bits
Spanner
Mitre saw (optional)
Orbital sander (or rough grade glasspaper)

MATERIALS

Exterior-grade transparent wood
   preservative
Seven lengths 193 cm (76 in) scaffold board
Four 64 cm (25^1/$_4$ in) lengths 75 mm (3 in)
   square sawn timber (legs)
Two 23 cm (9 in) lengths 50 mm (2 in)
   square sawn timber (seat supports)
Selection 75 mm (3 in) wood screws
Two 150 cm (60 in) lengths 75 mm (3 in)
   square sawn timber (top supports)
Four 10 cm (4 in) coach screws
Two pieces 20 cm x 20 cm x 5 cm
   (8 in x 8 in x 2 in) sawn timber
White emulsion paint (or selected colour
   multi-surface paint or stain)

The inspiration for this bench came from our stay at a holiday villa in Italy. Dug into the patio gravel, the legs were extended to support a pergola on which grew a glorious shading vine. The bench, far longer than the example in this project, soon became the the focal point for lazy lunches and long balmy evenings. A memorable holiday.

Tired of most of the benches so often seen in pubs and picnic areas, we decided to construct a scaled-down version of the Italian original without its roof, large enough to seat eight people, but just light enough to be moved around if wanted. The bench can be made to almost any size, its length extended by joining boards together and adding further support frames as required.

If you choose to make a static bench, the measurement of the legs should be extended to allow at least 20 cm (8 in) to be inserted in the ground. We used old fencing posts for the frame but rough sawn timber can be used instead. Before you start the construction of your bench, measure and record the width and thickness of the boards you will be using – we used scaffold boards which measured 23 cm (9 in) x 45 mm (1^3/$_4$ in). This measurement will be useful when calculating table top and seat heights, normally 76 cm (30 in) and 45 cm (18 in) respectively, and how many boards will be required for its top.

SCAFFOLD BENCH

METHOD

Treat all the wood used to make the bench with outdoor transparent wood preservative. Any cut surfaces should be similarly treated as the construction proceeds.

1 Mark a point 45 cm (18 in) from the bottom of one of the legs to represent the eventual height of the seat off the ground. Mark a second point the thickness of the scaffold board down from the first point, and a third point 50 mm (2 in) further down from the second point. Use the try square and pencil or marker pen to draw horizontal lines across one face at the second and third points. Extend each line by 25 mm (1 in) across the two adjacent faces of the leg. Join the ends of the two 25 mm (1 in) lines to mark out the area of the leg to be cut out to create a rebate for the seat support. Use the hand saw to cut along the marked sides of the rebate then remove the wood with a hammer and wood chisel. Repeat the process for the other three legs.

2 Mark the centre of one of the seat supports and insert the support into the rebate of a leg. Make sure the support is placed centrally and the joint fits tightly. Check the joint is square and secure the support in place with two 75 mm (3 in) wood screws. Repeat with the remaining three legs and seat supports.

3 It may be a good idea before proceeding further to lay out the four legs and two frame cross-members on a level surface to familiarise yourself with the construction sequence. Take one of the top supports and using the try square draw a line 75 mm (3 in) from one end. Mark a point centred between the line and the end of the top support and pre-

drill a hole for a coach screw. Repeat for the other end of the top support. Place one end of the top support over the top of a leg, insert a coach screw into the pre-drilled hole, and secure it to the leg using the spanner. Secure the other end of the top support to a second leg to complete assembly of the first frame. Make up the second frame with the remaining top support and two legs.

4 Use the hand saw (or mitre saw) to cut the two 20 cm x 20 cm x 5 cm (8 in x 8 in x 2 in) pieces of sawn timber in half diagonally to create four triangular corner braces. Check the assembled frames are square and fit the corner braces into position with 75 mm (3 in) wood screws. If you cannot find 20 cm x 20 cm x 5 cm (8 in x 8 in x 2 in) timber, you can use a brace made from 50 mm (2 in) or 75 mm (3 in) square timber with the ends cut at 45 degrees as an alternative.

5 Mark the central point of one end of one of the scaffold boards and a further two points 38 mm (1½ in) either side of the central point. Using the try square, draw lines through the second and third points, continuing them around the end onto the bottom of the board to a depth of 75 mm (3 in) on each surface. Join the ends of the 75 cm (3 in) lines to create the outline of a 75 mm (3 in) square rebate which will fit tightly over the leg. Cut out the marked rebate with the saw, hammer and chisel. Repeat for the other end of the board and both ends of a second board to create the two bench seats. Place the seats over the seat supports attached to the legs with the rebate fitted over the leg and fix in place with 75 mm (3 in) wood screws.

6 The bench frame should now be self-supporting. Place it on a level surface and mark the centres of the two top supports and the centre of both ends of a scaffold board. Use the marked points to locate the scaffold board centrally on the top supports and fix in place with one 75 mm (3 in) wood screw at each end. Double-check the angles with the try square and secure in place with two further screws at each end. Fit the remaining four boards into place butted either side of the central board and the structure of your bench is complete. Tighten all screws to make sure the bench is rigid.

7 Paint the entire bench with a coat of white emulsion diluted to half strength with water and leave to dry. (Multi-surface garden paint or stain can be used instead of emulsion depending on the colour finish you want. The Italian bench we so admired was stained black.)

8 When the paint is completely dry, sand with the orbital sander or glasspaper to remove the surface of the paint and reveal some of the underlying timber. Smooth off any rough timber or splinters, paying particular attention to sharp edges and areas where natural wear would occur. The bench is now ready to use.

CHEESE PRESS TABLE

EQUIPMENT

Wire brush
Rubber gloves
Stiff-bristled paintbrush
Small discardable paintbrush
Tape measure
Wood saw
Garden spade
Hand trowel
Metal or wooden rammer
Hammer

MATERIALS

Wooden cheese-press followers
Exterior-grade transparent wood
    preservative
Wood hardener
Logs
A number of 15 cm (6 in) galvanised
    round head nails

METHOD

1 Take the wooden cheese-press followers and remove any very soft or extraneous rotten wood using the wire brush. Place the followers on a flat surface and saturate them with transparent wood preservative using the stiff-bristled paintbrush. Make sure the entire surface of the wood is treated and allow the preservative to soak into the wood. Leave to dry. Apply a generous coating of wood hardener with the disposable paintbrush, ensuring that any particularly soft areas are saturated. Again, leave to dry.

2 Select the logs you will be using for the furniture stands, which should be at least 20 cm (8 in) longer than the desired table or seat height. Saw one end of each log straight across. Decide on the position for the furniture. For each table or seat, dig a hole at least 20 cm (8 in) deep where the stand will be inserted and remove any remaining soil with the hand trowel. Place the post into the hole with the cut end uppermost and horizontal and replace the soil, firming it with the metal or wooden rammer until the post is firmly held in position.

3 Place each cheese-press follower on the cut end of a post, making sure it is supported at its centre and secure in place with at least three 15 cm (6 in) galvanised nails. We selected 'green' or newly cut willow logs for the table supports and there is every chance that the willow will 'strike' and sprout new growth in years to come.

Safety note

We advise that rubber or protective gloves are used when applying timber preservative or hardener. Some formulations can be harmful: follow the manufacturers' instructions for application.

Cheesemaking was once an important rural industry. Surplus summer milk was turned into cheese as food for the winter and as a vital source of income.

Slow-maturing Cheddar, named after the north Somerset village, was the best known of the local cheeses. Although still made locally, Cheddar has become the generic name of what are often bad mimicries of the original farmhouse product.

Today, cheesemaking is no longer part of twenty-first century farm life and old, fancifully embellished, cast-iron cheese presses can still be snapped up at farm sales by collectors. The circular wooden press followers ('vollows' in local dialect), usually made of elm, are much more common. Made in different dimensions to suit the size of cheese being pressed, these wooden discs can often be found discarded, their origin unrecognised.

Over the years we have accumulated a number of wooden followers and have been seeking a practical use for some of the more worm-eaten and less well-preserved examples. Offcuts left from the pollarding of willow trees gave us the timber to convert our cheese press followers into garden seats and tables.

CHAIR PLANTER

EQUIPMENT

Pliers
Screwdriver
Marker pen
Metal or tin snips
Metal rule or straight edge
Heavy-duty craft knife
Electric drill and small metal bit

MATERIALS

Chair with seat rebate
Sheet zinc
25 mm (1 in) woodscrews

Almost any household will have one or two odd or mismatched unwanted chairs – if not, you will probably discover one in the first skip you see. Seats of many woven or upholstered chairs are removable and such chairs are ideal for this project. In our furniture design work we make a number of prototype chairs and the one used for this project is a beech chair which never went into production.

Chairs make effective and attractive planters which can be easily moved around the garden or patio. The one we made for this project is decorative, but we have made others with a more robust tray support, planted them with fragrant herbs such as thyme or camomile, and used them as practical occasional seats in the garden. Any shallow-rooted herb which is suitable for planting in a path or patio can be used but, because of the planter's shallow tray, frequent watering is essential.

We settled on a simple one-colour display for our planter but a striking effect can be achieved by using plants of different size and colour and embellishing the chair with planted flower pots hung from its back. We decided to make a shallow frame for our chair planter which would be concealed within the seat frame. If you choose to construct yours with a deeper tray to hold a greater reserve of soil or planting medium you could plant it with hanging plants to conceal its base.

CHAIR PLANTER

METHOD

The chair we selected for this project was neither painted nor treated and since we designed it for only occasional outside use we decided to leave it that way. If you propose to leave your planter outside, treat the chair with a timber preservative or exterior-grade timber paint before use. There are a number of attractively coloured paints and preservatives now on the market, ideal for this purpose.

1 Remove the seat from the chair frame and take off any wooden supports with the pliers or screwdriver. Place the chair upside down on top of the zinc sheet on the edge of a work surface and draw around the inside of the seat with the marker pen.

2 Measure the depth of the seat rebate and add to this an extra 50 mm (2 in). Draw a second line, to the distance of this combined measurement, around the existing shape on the zinc sheet. Cut to size with the metal snips. Cut a rectangle from each corner from the marked seat size to the outside with the metal snips to allow the zinc sheet to be bent into a tray shape. Use the heavy-duty craft knife and metal rule or straight edge to lightly score along the marked lines outlining the shape of the seat. Turn the sheet over and score along the second and outside marked lines.

3 Place the zinc sheet on the work surface, with the scored lines of the seat shape uppermost. Gently bend each side of the sheet over the work surface edge to form a tray shape to fit inside the seat rebate. Use the work surface edge to gently bend the outside scored lines to a right-angle to create a lip around the tray to hold it securely within the seat rebate.

4 Place the completed tray on a piece of scrap timber and use the electric drill and metal drill bit to drill a series of drainage holes in the base. Drill a further two holes in each flap to allow the tray to be securely screwed into position within the seat rebate.

5 Place the tray into the seat rebate and secure in place with two 25 mm (1 in) screws driven through each flap into the seat surround. Fill the tray within the assembled chair planter with soil or planting medium and plant with your selected flowers or herbs. Press down the soil around the plants and thoroughly water before placing the planter in position.

POTTING STAND

EQUIPMENT

Paintbrush
Tape measure
Try square
Pencil or marker
Hand saw
Electric drill and wood bit
Electric (or hand) screwdriver

MATERIALS

Colourless timber preservative
Selection 30 mm (1¼ in) wood screws
Selection 50 mm (2 in) wood screws

TIMBER

For the base:

75 mm (3 in) square softwood timber
    cut into:
    Two front legs approx. 71 cm (28 in)
    Two rear legs approx. 112 cm (44 in)
10 cm (4 in) x 2 cm (³⁄₄ in) softwood timber
    cut into:
    Two side stretchers approx. 60 cm
    (23½ in)
    One rear stretcher approx. 93 cm
    (36½ in)
22 cm (9 in) x 2 cm (³⁄₄ in) softwood timber
    cut into:
    Two bin sides approx. 60 cm (23½ in)
    One bin front approx. 97 cm (38 in)
Quantity approx. 25 mm (1 in) square
    softwood (support battens)
15 cm (6 in) x 12 mm (½ in) softwood
    timber cut into:
    Two pot boards approx. 93 cm (36½ in)
One piece 12 mm (½ in) waterproof
    plywood or particle board approx.
    93 cm (36½ in) x 60 cm (23¾ in)
    (bin base)

For the top:

20 cm (8 in) x 2 cm (³⁄₄ in) softwood timber
    cut into:
    Two side pieces approx. 89 cm (35 in)
    One bottom shelf approx. 93 cm
    (36½ in)
    One vertical divider approx. 60 cm
    (23⅝ in)
    One long shelf approx. 61 cm (24 in)
    One short shelf approx. 30 cm (11¾ in)
One approx. 98 cm (38½ in) length 22 cm
    (9 in) x 2 cm (³⁄₄ in) softwood timber
    (top piece)
Seven approx. 112 cm (44 in) lengths 15 cm
    (6 in) x 2 cm (³⁄₄ in) softwood timber
    (back boards)

A potting shed is not only the focus of propagating activities necessary for the cultivation of a well managed garden, but if insulated and properly equipped can also be a cool retreat in summer and a cosy refuge in winter. Away from the accusing eyes of neglected roses and a vista of unmown grass, it can become a comfortable bolt hole for all but the most conscientious of gardeners – a private sanctuary where peace and quiet reign, the demanding shrill of the telephone remains unheard, and the mindless chatter of television and the clamour of much-loved children can be ignored. The perfect environment for indulgence in slow, deep and somnolent thought.

Unfortunately, such escapism demands a price. A potting shed needs a potting stand to justify your time spent in it, and ours is ideal. The bin holds sufficient compost for almost every job, the shelved back accommodates pots, packets of seed and other miscellanea, and the pot board underneath provides extra vital storage space. If desired, a plank or board can be laid over the compost bin to make a surface perfect for those other gardening necessities – a book, a cup of tea or perhaps a glass of whisky!

Made from salvaged fence posts and reclaimed roofing softwood, the stand can be simply disassembled for installation where there is restricted access, or should you need to move it at a later date.

POTTING STAND

METHOD

Before assembling the potting stand, paint all the timber you will be using for this project with colourless timber preservative. Pay particular attention to sawn ends and end grain.

1 Lay one front and one rear leg on a flat surface, the front on the left and the rear on the right. On the uppermost faces of each leg, measure two points 20 cm (8 in) and 63 cm (24³/₄ in) from the bottom of the leg. Use the try square and pencil to draw horizontal lines at each of these points. Place a side stretcher across the bottom line of both legs and a bin side on the top line and secure in place with 50 mm (2 in) wood screws. Repeat with the other two legs, but this time place the front leg on the right and the rear leg on the left to create the two opposing side frames.

2 Turn the side frames over and fit a length of batten to the inside of each bin side, one end flush with and butted against the top of the front leg the other approximately 25 mm (1 in) short of the rear leg. Place the two sides upright with their rear legs flat on the surface and the side stretchers and bin sides on the outside. Fit the rear stretcher across the rear legs inside the bin sides, its top level with the top of the battens. Screw securely in place with 50 mm (2 in) wood screws.

3 Place the bin front over the front legs, its ends flush with the outside faces of the bin sides, and secure in place with 50 mm (2 in) wood screws. Turn the base over onto its front and fit a length of batten to the rear of the bin front between and flush with the tops of the front legs. You have now made the basic structure of the potting stand base.

4 Stand the base upright on its legs and, checking the frame is square, fit the two pot boards over the side stretchers, butting them against the back legs. Fix in place with 50 mm (2 in) screws.

5 Carefully measure the inside dimensions of the open-backed bin you have made and cut the waterproof plywood or particle board to that size, removing a notch from each back corner to fit over the rear legs. Drop into place so that it rests on the battens, the front legs and the top of the rear stretcher, and secure in place with 30 mm (1¹/₄ in) wood screws. The potting stand base is now complete.

6 You are now ready to start construction of the potting-stand top. First check the measurement between the outsides of the rear legs of the base. Depending on the thickness of the timber you have used for the base construction, this should be approximately 93 cm (36¹/₂ in). This measurement is important as the top is designed to fit snugly over the rear legs (which are raised above the top of the base) and rest on the bin sides. Measure a point 26 cm (10¹/₄ in) from the bottom of each side piece and draw across with the pencil and try square. Fit the bottom shelf between the two side pieces level with that marked point and secure it to them with 50 mm (2 in) wood screws. Take the top piece and place it on top of the side pieces with an overhang at the sides and front and fit it in place with 50 mm (2 in) wood screws. You have now constructed the basic frame of the top. Mark a point 30 cm (11³/₄ in) from one end on both the top piece and the bottom shelf. Fit the vertical divider at that point with 5 cm (2 in)

screws to divide the frame into two unequal sections. Mark points just above halfway on the inside of the vertical divider and side piece within the wider section and fit the long shelf in position. Finally mark points approximately 4 cm (1¹/₂ in) above the long shelf on the inside of the remaining smaller section and fit the short shelf at that position.

7 Place the assembled top structure face down on the surface, check it is square and starting at one side with the edge of the first back board flush with the outside face of the side piece, proceed to attach the remaining back boards to the rear, securing with 50 mm (2 in) screws. It may be necessary to cut the final board down to fit. Carefully lift the completed top section onto the base so that it fits over the extended back legs and the side pieces rest on the bin sides. Secure with screws driven through the back boards into the legs and rear edge of the bin sides. Place in position, fill the bin with potting compost and your potting stand is ready for use.

CONCRETE TABLE

EQUIPMENT

Pointing trowel
Shovel
Cement-mixing board or wheelbarrow
Club hammer
Spirit level
Tape measure
Soft hand brush
Paintbrush (optional)

MATERIALS

Soft building sand
Cement
Mortar plasticiser (optional)
Approximately ten 15 cm (6 in)
    concrete blocks
Concrete slab top
Multi-surface garden or masonry paint
    (optional)

METHOD

If the garden table is to be built on a solid surface, clean it of any lichen or other growth. On a new site, it must be laid on a concrete foundation (one part cement to two parts soft sand and four parts aggregate) at least 30 cm (12 in) deep. The base should be allowed to harden before the plinth is installed. Calculate how many blocks will be required to construct a plinth of the right height for the table. Table tops are normally approximately 76 cm (30 in) high. Remember to allow for the thickness of the top and each layer of mortar.

1 Place two concrete blocks approximately 20 mm (³/₄ in) apart on the ground where the table plinth will be built. Draw around them with the point of your trowel and put the blocks to one side. Make up a workable mortar mix of five parts soft building sand to one part cement and water and place a thick layer of the mix inside the trowel marks. Replace the two blocks in position on the mortar and tap into place with the handle of the trowel or club hammer, periodically checking the spirit level. Clean off excess mortar from around the base and use it to fill the joint between the two blocks. Do not fill the gap completely as this may cause them to splay.

2 Place the next two blocks at right-angles to the first course. Apply mortar across one end of both blocks sufficient for one of the blocks on the second course. Tap the block into place, checking that it is level and that the sides are vertical. Place mortar on the remainder of the first course and lay the fourth block alongside the one you have just laid. Fill the outside of the vertical joint and smooth to a good finish.

3 Continue building up the plinth to the desired height, checking the levels as you go. To fit the top, place mortar around the edge of the top course and a trowelful in the centre. Fit the top carefully on the mortar, and when centred make sure it is entirely level. Tap it firmly in place with the handle of the club hammer. Remove excess mortar from around the top of the plinth. After about four hours, brush over joints with a soft brush to give a smooth finish and remove any loose material. Keep new blockwork moist in hot weather and protect from sun, wind, rain or frost with a sheet of polythene. Allow one week for the mortar to fully cure before using the table. If desired, the plinth can be painted with two coats of multi-surface garden paint or masonry paint, applied with a stiff brush.

Alfresco dining is one of life's great pleasures. Whilst any number of portable tables can be taken into the garden for an impromptu occasion, a properly designed and constructed table, erected where it will be constantly used, is very convenient. Before you build a permanent table in your garden or on your patio, we suggest you erect a temporary mock-up in the proposed position to make sure the site is suitable. Once built, it will be a lasting feature.

During inclement weather the table can be used for arrangements of plants in pots or urns, or for an outdoor sculpture. It will become a feature of the garden, as much appreciated when not in use as when it is the venue for outdoor entertaining.

Finding a table top of a suitable size can be a problem. Surfaces can be made of timber or even heavy glass, but we made this one from the side of an old concrete coal bunker which had become redundant. The side was extremely heavy, requiring at least two people to move it, and the bolt holes in its corners required filling with a sand and cement mixture. However, it had the considerable advantage of being robust and its bevelled edge made it particularly suitable as a table top. Large stones, slate or concrete paving slabs could be used as other alternatives.

PLANTS, PLANTERS AND PLANTING

It is so easy to drive down to the local garden centre, load up the trolley and buy all the containers needed for use in the garden – as easy, in fact, as going to the supermarket for the weekly food shopping. Although there is always a good selection of mass-produced pots and troughs to choose from, at varying price levels, the one thing they lack is individuality. So next time you are tempted to jump in the car en route to the garden centre, just stop for a moment and think about what you may already have lying around that could so easily be recycled.

Check in the garden shed, look at the back of the garage or investigate the unsightly pile at the front of the house awaiting a trip to the rubbish dump. Put aside old terracotta piping, metal buckets of differing sizes, concrete blocks and wooden packing cases, in fact anything which looks as if it could contain plants or shrubs and withstand having holes drilled in it for drainage. You will be astonished at just how much can be 'repurposed' to become something both useful and decorative, giving new colour, texture and shape to a garden.

Container gardening has many advantages, not least versatility, particularly in areas where restricted space limits the number of plants that can be accommodated, such as small town gardens, roof gardens and balconies. Planting in containers allows for a garden to be changed with the seasons. The planters can be easily moved around, repositioned if the plants need more light or shade, or built up on supports to give the display height and structure. Species intolerant of cold can be grown outside in pots to give colour through the summer months, then brought inside with the approach of colder weather. Grow herbs in pipes pushed into the soil and arranged artistically.

Raised beds are often used to grow neat rows of green cabbages, winter spinach, lettuce, chard and other vegetables together with swirls of sage, parsley and camomile. They answer the problems posed by limited space and are useful if you want to grow acid-loving plants in a lime-rich garden. Raised beds allow the soil to heat up faster, are easily maintained and can be made quite small if necessary. They can be constructed from a wide choice of materials, but old railway sleepers look suitably informal and can be found via the classified section of the local newspaper, farming magazines or reclamation dealers.

Certain plants which have a tendency to get out of control, such as mint, can be planted in plastic or metal buckets dug into the earth. A disused and bottomless metal dustbin or two old tyres piled on top of one another to contain the growth of rhubarb need not look unsightly if painted in an old-fashioned dark green or other subdued colour to blend with the planting. Why not choose primary colours of red, blue and yellow, just for a bit of fun! Continue the theme by transforming salvaged oil drums, large wooden litter bins, metal feed troughs, cans, drainpipes and cast-iron guttering with bright paint colours. Although painting containers is rather obvious, it gives an instant, easy and inexpensive effect which will lift the spirits and introduce life to a boring back yard.

FAR LEFT

A carved stone feeding trough in the garden of a retired farming couple was once in use in the cattle yard of their former farm. Eight men were needed to carry it to the garden of their present home. Old stone troughs are much in demand and fetch high prices at garden antique auctions.

BELOW LEFT

Tripod legs have been secured to a weathered log to make a rustic plant-stand used to conceal an unsightly drain cover in this urban garden.

CENTRE LEFT

Ancient brick door leading from the walled White Garden to the productive kitchen gardens at Birtsmorton Court. The terracotta urns and plinths blend with the old mellow brick wall perfectly.

BELOW RIGHT

Old slate used as edging to retain a bed of flowering culinary herbs beside the kitchen garden at the retreat, Emmaüs House.

NEAR LEFT

An established wisteria has been trained to grow on supports made from timber salvaged from disused wooden pallets and mounted on a stone wall facing the kitchen window of garden enthusiasts Ron and Judy Mathews.

LEFT

A typical wooden framed farmhouse in Normandy, France showing the thatched roof capped with a traditional mixture of succulents, lilies and grasses and its gable end adorned with a glorious miscellany of summer flowers in a variety of salvaged containers.

PACKING CASE PLANTER

EQUIPMENT

Claw hammer
Pliers
Wood saw
Scissors
Staple gun
Craft knife

MATERIALS

Wooden packing case
Scrap timber or plywood
25 mm (1 in) panel pins or thin nails
Quantity of fine-mesh garden netting
  or hessian
Heavy duty staples to fit staple gun

The current demand for ceramic pots, vases and bowls has resulted in innumerable fragile vessels being imported from all corners of the world, many packed in wooden boxes or crates to protect them during their travels. We have long been aware of the potential of these crates as a ready and inexpensive source of sometimes quite exotic timbers. We used a crate found outside a gift shop and made of wooden branches lashed together with rawhide to make a stunning coffee table when surmounted with polished packing case timber. We salvaged Brazilian mahogany used to pack machine parts and complete with its original stencilled shipping marks to construct table tops and benches.

Keep your eyes open for discarded materials which may have been used for a quite utilitarian original purpose, but which can be salvaged and transformed into something surprising and exotic. The packing cases we found for these planters were discovered in a well known store. Used to hold glazed pots, they were about to be put out with the shop's refuse. The store manager was only too glad to let us take them away.

Disposal of unwanted packaging is an increasing problem for retailers who are generally very willing to find an alternative use for it. Damaged or broken pallets are an excellent source of timber and by being prepared to sort and collect it ourselves, we seldom have to purchase new boxes or packaging for the furniture we make and sell.

PACKING CASE PLANTER

METHOD

1 Place the packing case on a convenient surface and remove any lid or protruding nails or staples with the claw hammer and pliers.

2 Turn the case upside down. Cut pieces of scrap timber or plywood to fill any gaps in the base of the case. Secure with panel pins or nails to make a solid floor to the planter.

3 Cut the fine-mesh garden netting, or hessian, into four pieces to match the shapes of the sides of the box. Use these to line the interior of the planter, fixing them in place with the staple gun and staples.

4 Fill the planter halfway with planting medium. Using the scissors or craft knife, cut crosses through the garden netting at places where you want plants to grow sideways through the planter. Gently insert the plants through the netting into the medium. Complete the planting from the top of the case. We used a selection of culinary herbs for this planter but almost any plants can be used. Water well and, when drained, place the planter in its selected position. If you wish, you can convert this planter into a hanging basket by attaching screw eyes and chain to each corner.

CAST-IRON BOILER PLANTER

EQUIPMENT

Wire brush
Electric drill and high-speed drill bit
  (optional)

MATERIALS

Copper or cast-iron boiler
Chimneypot

METHOD

1 Clean the boiler with the wire brush to remove any extraneous rust. Similarly clean the chimneypot of any cement or mortar and unsightly stains. Should you wish to plant directly into the boiler you will at this stage have to drill a drainage hole in the boiler's base, but as we chose to use an already planted pot for our display, this was unnecessary.

2 Place the chimneypot in position, making sure it is vertical and the top level. Carefully place the boiler on top of the chimneypot, taking care not to chip the top of the pot while centering the boiler and making it secure. Check that you are happy with the final height of the planter – we decided to put an extra piece of stone under the chimneypot to give the planter additional height. Plant as desired, or place an already planted arrangement in a plastic or similar container inside the boiler.

There are many locations within almost any garden where a fixed planter can be placed to advantage. An old well in front of our house, now long disused, has been covered with a stark and unsightly stone slab which dominates what was once a vegetable garden but is now laid to lawn. We have long been looking for a simple 'architectural' planter which could mask this stone and add a touch of drama to the garden. We experimented with a sundial but decided the area needed something else. A simple yet striking tall planter seemed to be the perfect solution and, having no better ideas, we decided to visit a local reclamation yard to seek inspiration.

Copper boilers are much sought after and expensive to buy if you are fortunate to find one, but the much more common cast-iron boiler was once a feature in almost every home and the focus for the thriving domestic activity which surrounded the weekly family wash. We found our boiler among a number of others in the yard, and nearby there were some ancient chimneypots, any one of which could have been used for this project.

WASTE BIN PLANTER

EQUIPMENT

Tape measure
Pencil
Ruler or straight edge
Wood saw
Hammer
Electric drill with small wood bit
Screwdriver
50 mm (2 in) paintbrush

MATERIALS

Quantity of marine or exterior-grade
   plywood
25 mm (1 in) panel pins or thin round
   head nails
Quantity of approximately 25 mm
   (1 in) square softwood timber
40 mm (1½ in) wood screws
Dark brown timber preservative

METHOD

Our waste bin was constructed of slatted wood fixed to a rigid timber framework and had been designed to hold a removable metal or plastic inner container which had long disappeared. Otherwise the bin was in an excellent state of preservation.

1 Measure the inside dimensions of the four sides of the bin and use the pencil and straight edge to draw out their shapes on the marine or exterior-grade plywood. Cut to shape with the wood saw and nail into place with the panel pins or round head nails.

2 Measure the depth of the plant container you will be placing in the bin and add approximately 50 mm (2 in) to give you the depth at which to fix the battens inside the bin. Measure across the inside of the bin at that length and cut two battens to that length from the 25 mm (1 in) square timber. Use the wood screws to fit the two battens on opposite sides to each other in the bin.

3 Measure the width across the newly fitted battens and cut three or four slats from the 25 mm (1 in) square timber to fit. Start holes with the electric drill and wood bit and secure slats in place with the 40 mm (1½ in) wood screws. Paint the whole planter with a liberal application of preservative, allow to dry and place your selected plant container on the slatted support.

We discovered this wooden bin in our local waste and recycling depot. The bin had been discarded and its metal liner had long gone missing but its shape suggested a new life as an imposing planter. We soon discovered a second matching waste bin, this one complete with a plaque proclaiming 'Place Litter Inside', which we speedily removed and installed on the outside of our teenage daughter's bedroom.

Large planters are essential for some plants and planting schemes and these waste bins were perfect for the site and plants we had selected, requiring very little conversion. Their construction is so simple that we have subsequently made up several more in different sizes for a patio town garden.

The original waste bin was aged and very faded and we decided to smarten it with a coat of dark brown wood preservative to give it a new lease of life. There is no reason why such bins cannot be finished with a transparent timber preservative if the original look is to be maintained, or tranformed with a coat of one of the many coloured wood paints and preservatives now commercially available.

It is said that gardens and gardening are good for the soul and many a city dweller craves their own piece of private, outdoor space. However small – whether it is a roof terrace, or a seen on our television screens in recent times. As a result, instant gardens fashionably furnished with wooden decking, terracotta pots and architectural, foreign plants have become top of the

A GARDEN RECLAIMED

patio just big enough for a barbecue, or a balcony decked with pot plants – it is somewhere to potter with a trowel in the open air, an essential sanctuary in which to just sit and think. This trend towards outdoor living has been fed by the plethora of garden make-over programmes must-have list for many people. In reality gardens are not instant but evolve over time and need some looking after, however low-maintenance the design may be. If at any stage it is redesigned, the plan will usually incorporate many of the existing plants, shrubs and trees.

LEFT

An informal arrangement of
damaged nineteenth-century
terracotta pots almost
overwhelmed by succulents
in the Abbey Gardens, Tresco.

RIGHT

A superb example of an
original Victorian greenhouse,
rescued from dereliction by
John Nelson and re-erected
at The Lost Gardens of
Heligan in Cornwall.

In this chapter we have taken a small garden which had fallen into neglect and transformed it, working as much as possible with what was already there. As lovage, fennel and a border of piercing, purplish-blue catmint were already there, they made an obvious starting point in the plan to establish a fragrant herb garden which would be sweetly scented on summer evenings, give some greenery all year round and provide delicious herbs for culinary use. The herb garden would enclose a crazy-paved area using stones salvaged from the garden and softened by more herbs growing between the slabs. Yet more herbs were planted into a few clay drainage pipes (pots could be used) to achieve extra height and structure. Reached by four stone steps edged with wooden railway sleepers, the design incorporated various edgings of terracotta and slate tiles, railway sleeper blocks and old mellow bricks, with slate chippings and tiny pebbles used as mulches, all suited to small areas.

Two other features were deemed essential: the soothing sound of water and a table for alfresco dining. An old cattle water trough was bought which made an ideal container,

NEAR LEFT

Gravel steps leading from the patio area through a rose covered pergola to the garden beyond have been constructed from crushed stone gravel behind salvaged slate and treated timber log retainers.

BOTTOM LEFT

Interior of the orange house in the Lost Gardens of Heligan showing detail of the restored timber framing and beaver-tail glass, some rescued from collapsed buildings on the site and some made to the original pattern.

BOTTOM RIGHT

Steps lead from the patio outside garden designer Sarah Gidden's house in a small market town and up to a pathway constructed of reclaimed bricks and pavement stone. The central feature was rescued in pieces by Sarah's antique dealer husband and carefully reinstalled to create a focal point to this garden 'room'.

painted a dark green colour to blend in with the planting. An inexpensive fountain pump was fitted in the water and the trough planted with striking yellow irises found abandoned on the roadside after ditches had been cleared. The table was constructed, its top made of the concrete side of a coal bunker and the base from breeze blocks.

Before the garden came to fruition much groundwork needed to be done. The soil had to be excavated and several loads disposed of, revealing a stony sub-structure and quite a lot of rubbish. This was nothing compared to the garden we had acquired with our rundown farmhouse which, once rotavated, produced enough stones, flint, broken terracotta, baling twine, coloured plastic, polystyrene, old bones, rusty metal, decomposing leather, shards of glass and china chips to fill a disused quarry.

It was the bits of broken china that first caught the eye. Blue and white seemed to predominate, especially willow pattern which was commonly used for everyday ware. A fascination, or perhaps one should say obsession, began to gain a grip, making a journey to the compost heap or washing line impossible without eyes glued to the ground in search of treasure. And then the joy of finding some in shades of blue ranging from pale pastels through bright cobalt to inky blacks; large pieces and small, all caked in grime, until the collection filled three empty shoe boxes. One day in the dim and distant future, when leisure allows, they will be used to cover the concrete table, making a magnificent mosaic.

EDGING BRICKS

EQUIPMENT

Pointing trowel
Garden spade
Shovel
Cement-mixing board or wheelbarrow
String line and pegs
Spirit level
Hand brush

MATERIALS

Quantity old bricks
Broken stone
Cement
Sharp builders' sand
Aggregate

METHOD

Carefully select the bricks you will use for this project. As they will be laid on edge, ensure that at least one edge is sound and remove any extraneous mortar with the trowel. If you are using different coloured bricks or the sizes vary slightly, mix them well before laying in order to achieve a uniform appearance. Put aside any mortar removed from the bricks and add it to the broken stone to be laid in the base of the trench.

1 Excavate a trench 25 cm (10 in) deep the entire length of the proposed edging border. Fill the trench with a 10 cm (4 in) layer of compacted broken stone. On the mixing board or wheelbarrow, use the shovel to make a dry mixture of one part cement to three parts sharp sand and six parts aggregate. Cover the stone base with the dry mix to a depth of about 10 cm (4 in). Using the string and pegs to give you a straight line, lay the bricks on their edges on the dry mix, each approximately 12 mm (^{1}/$_2$ in) apart. Tap the bricks into the bed of dry mix with the handle of the trowel, checking the level with the spirit level.

2 Make another dry mix, this time with one part cement to four parts dry soft sand, and use it to fill the joints between the laid bricks, removing any excess mortar with the brush.

3 Try to compact the mortar with the trowel and brush when the bricks are being laid. Cover with plastic sacks or a waterproof cover to protect from rain and leave for at least forty-eight hours for the mix to take up moisture from the soil and atmosphere until it completely hardens. By using a dry mix to lay the edging bricks, you will minimise any cement staining or unsightly spillage.

Old bricks are probably the most commonly reclaimed building material. Usually known as 'old stock' bricks, they are required for much building work undertaken in areas where new constructions must match the existing architecture. Of greater interest to us is the ready availability of old bricks, even when they require some cleaning to remove old mortar before they can be reused.

Old bricks have a charm, individuality and character almost entirely lacking in their modern counterparts, ranging in colour from blue, almost purple, to yellow and in hardness from the granite-like density of some engineering and stable bricks to the soft crumbly texture of many low-fired handmade stocks. Despite their obvious attractiveness, most old bricks from demolition work are still taken to landfill sites as the labour required to sort, clean and find a market for them outweighs their commercial value.

We are active skip-watchers, and always keep our eyes open for materials to liberate. We recently managed to retrieve a large number of bricks from restoration work being undertaken to a local department store. The bricks, mostly in excellent condition, were being loaded into a skip before being taken to landfill and the site foreman was more than happy to allow us to remove those we wanted to salvage.

Brick is an obvious and practical solution for 'hard' garden edging and those we rescued proved ideal for this project.

SLEEPER AND STONE STEPS

EQUIPMENT

Tape measure
Chain saw or cross-cut saw
Garden spade
Shovel
Wheelbarrow
Cement-mixing board
Club hammer
Bolster or stone chisel
Spirit level
Pointing trowel
Hand brush
Watering can

MATERIALS

Quantity paving stone
Quantity railway sleepers
Large quantity of broken stone
   or rubble
Cement
Sharp builders' sand
Aggregate
Selection scrap wood

Safety note

As using a chain saw is dangerous, it is advised
that eye protection and a dust mask are worn.
Eye protection should always be used if stone
is being cut with a club hammer and bolster.

For years the only access to our
raised garden had been an agile
leap from some old stone steps at
the end of a path, which had once
led into the adjoining property,
onto a pile of concrete blocks and
from these onto the garden which
was about a metre (3 feet) above
the level of the path. Not an
entirely practical arrangement,
especially when laden with home-
grown produce or carrying a
watering can or garden tools.

Steps leading from the path
to the level of the planned crazy-
paved surface of our new patio
garden were essential. Steps must
be both practical and safe. Their
width may be dictated by the site,
and the number of steps needed
by the height and the material you
will be using for the risers. We
were fortunate to have a number
of short lengths of railway
sleepers, given to us by a
neighbouring farmer, which we
had left over from various other
projects we had constructed
around our garden. We wanted
the steps to blend with the
colours and textures of our
garden and so decided to make
the treads of our steps with
paving stone to match the
existing stone retaining walls
of the raised garden.

SLEEPER AND STONE STEPS

METHOD

Select the stone you will be using for this project. Look for stones of a similar size and depth and make sure each stone has at least one good surface. Reject any which are flaking or crumbling. Measure the width of the steps you will be building and cut the sleepers to that length with the chain saw.

1 Select a quantity of paving stones of approximately equal size and depth sufficient to cover the proposed tread area of the steps and put to one side. The height (rise) and depth (tread) of the step will be dependent on whether you propose to use the sleepers on edge or flat. Normally the rise should be 15 to 20 cm (6 to 8 in) and the tread should be twice that measurement. Calculate how many steps will be required by dividing the height of the slope where the steps are to be built by the measurement of a single riser. Dig out the first step to the dimension of the tread but excavate a further 15 cm (6 in) at the front, as a footing on which the sleeper riser will be laid.

2 Fill the bottom 10 cm (4 in) of the footing with compacted broken stone or rubble. On the mixing board or in the wheelbarrow, make a mortar mix of one part cement to four parts sharp sand and sufficient water to make a firm mix and use it to cover the broken stone in the footing to a further depth of about 5 cm (2 in). Lay a cut sleeper on the mix, tap it into place with the club hammer and check it with the spirit level. Cover against rain and leave to dry for at least twenty-four hours. When dry, fill

the excavated space behind the riser with more compacted stone and rubble up to approximately 10 cm (4 in) of its top. Make up a further mortar mix, but this time dry (without water), place over the compacted stone, and bed your paving stones into it so that their surface is level with the top of the sleeper riser.

3 Lay each paving stone down with a screwing motion to ensure that it is securely bedded and will not rock or move, adding or removing dry mix as required. Try to keep the gaps between stones as small as possible – if necessary, the paving stones can be cut to size with the club hammer and bolster. Use the hammer cushioned with a scrap of waste timber to tap the stones into place. When the paving is laid and levelled to your satisfaction, use more of the dry mortar mix to fill the joints. Press down the mixture between the joints with a scrap of wood to compact it and use the brush to clean off any debris and surplus dry mortar mix from the paving surface. The dry mix will normally take up moisture from the soil and atmosphere but in dry weather curing will be aided by sprinkling water from a watering can fitted with a fine rose over the pointing. Cover and leave to set.

4 Repeat the above for each step, ensure that the level of the top of the last riser is finished flush with the proposed level of any new paving or surface. To construct the steps for our raised garden, we built a retaining side wall of reclaimed walling stone. We used a mortar mix of one part cement to one part soft sand and four parts stone dust. We use the stone dust in order to match the mortar used on the existing walls. The appearance of newly constructed steps can be softened by planting a few lime tolerant, low growing plants in soil-filled crevices left during construction.

STONE CRAZY PAVING

EQUIPMENT

Garden spade
Shovel
Wheelbarrow
Spirit level
String and pegs
Cement-mixing board
Club hammer
Bolster or stone chisel
Pointing trowel
Medium-bristled broom
Hand brush
Watering can (optional)

MATERIALS

Quantity paving stone
Large quantity of broken stone
    or rubble
Cement
Sharp builders' sand
Selection scrap wood

Safety note

Eye protection should always be used if stone is
being cut with a club hammer and bolster.

Our raised garden is the result of generations of former occupiers depositing their household rubbish and farming miscellanea. For the first few years after we bought the farmhouse we used the garden for growing vegetables and in the course of digging found fascinating evidence of the past. Shards of blue and white willow pattern crockery are now stored for future mosaics; remnants of salt-glazed pots and buckles from discarded harnesses told of earlier times; and on one occasion we even unearthed a brass cartridge case. Although it was fertile we felt this area was wasted and since it had been made redundant by a new kitchen garden we decided to create a paved sitting area where its west-facing aspect would allow us to enjoy the last evening light.

We live in an area where most houses are built of stone and the Draycott conglomerate used widely throughout the locality for pillars and gateposts and local blue lias used for flagstone floors are particularly in demand. Built on the site of a considerably older farmhouse, many of our outbuildings predate the house and a consequence of such extended occupation is the quantity of stone and other building materials to be found all over our garden hidden just under the soil. A useful building resource if not always an encouragement to cultivation.

Among the stone we have recovered from our garden is a considerable quantity of paving stone, some of which has been used for this project.

STONE CRAZY PAVING

METHOD

First make sure you have an adequate supply of reasonably large paving stones to cover the area you propose to pave. As far as possible select stones of an equal depth and make sure that one face of each stone is smooth and sound. Put aside stones with one straight edge as they will prove particularly useful as edging pieces.

1 Remove any weeds and debris from the area to be excavated, taking particular care to remove any roots.

2 Excavate the whole area with the garden spade and shovel to a depth of approximately 15 cm (6 in) plus the average depth of your selected paving below the final decided level. Compact loose soil and check that the area is almost level with the board and spirit level. Allow for a slight slope for drainage run-off.

3 If you have decided to border the paved area with beds or to create a complex shape, mark out the edges with string tied to pegs driven into the ground. Remove the soil excavated from the area. Some may usefully be retained for adding to the borders.

4 Fill the bottom 10 cm (4 in) of the excavated area with compacted broken stone or rubble. On the mixing board or in the wheelbarrow, use the shovel to make a dry mortar mix of one part cement to four parts sharp sand. Spread the dry mix over the broken stone to a depth of about 5 cm (2 in). Starting from one corner, lay the edging pieces first with the straight edge outwards adding further paving stones until the area is covered. Make sure all stones are securely bedded, adding or removing dry mix as required. Gaps between the stones should be small, and if necessary, cut paving stones to fit with the club hammer and bolster.

5 When the paving is laid to your satisfaction, sprinkle dry mortar mix over the area and use the broom to brush it into the joints. Compact the mortar between the joints with a scrap of wood and use the hand brush to clean off any surplus from the surface. In wet weather the dry mix will normally take up moisture from the soil and air but in dry conditions curing will be aided by sprinkling water from a watering can over the pointing. Cover the area to protect it from rain and leave to set.

EDGING SLATE & TILES

EQUIPMENT

Electric slate and tile cutter or disc cutter
Garden spade
String line and pegs
Shovel
Cement-mixing board or wheelbarrow
Hand brush
Pointing trowel
Spirit level
Club hammer

MATERIALS

Quantity broken slates and tiles
Broken stone
Cement
Sharp builders' sand
Aggregate
Length of scrap wood

Safety note

It is advised that eye protection and a dust mask
are worn if electrical cutting equipment is used.

Old tiles and slates together with reclaimed bricks are the life blood of most salvage yards. The variety of colour found in native and imported slate is almost bewildering and the range of sizes, colours and patterns in which tiles were made in the past means that matching old tiles can be quite difficult and time-consuming.

We have used slates and tiles in our garden for all sorts of purposes and have seen them used in numerous inventive ways in other gardens, both here and abroad. Old slates are an obvious choice for the roofing of garden structures, but they can also be used to cap a wall or to act as a hard-wearing flooring material. We use them buried deep into the soil to contain invasive plants in a border, and laid on edge, as we show in this project, they have a particularly attractive appearance. Tiles are just as useful. We know of one enterprising gardener who has built an entire garden bench from stacked Double Roman tiles. In the same garden, tiles have been laid to delineate paths and different beds.

In almost any reclamation yard you will find discarded and broken tiles or slates which can very often be had for the asking. There is something particularly satisfying in securing a useful material for nothing! We decided to make a border of mixed edging for our raised herb patio garden and managed to construct it entirely from old and broken slates and tiles from a local reclamation yard had just for the cost of collection.

EDGING SLATE & TILES

METHOD

As the slates and tiles will be laid on edge, make sure you have enough for the job. You will need approximately eight tiles or sixteen slates for each 15 cm (6 in) length of edging. Select slates and tiles at least 15 cm (6 in) long by at least 10 cm (4 in) wide. Use the slate and tile cutter to trim the pieces to a uniform length; the width can vary between 10 cm (4 in) and 15 cm (6 in) as this edge will be hidden below the surface.

1 Dig a trench approximately 25 cm (10 in) deep the entire length of the proposed edging. Insert the pegs at each end with the string stretched between them to act as a guide for laying the slates and tiles. Fill the trench with broken stone to a depth of approximately 10 cm (4 in) and compact it down to form a firm base.

2 On the mixing board or in the wheelbarrow, use the shovel to make a dry mixture of one part cement to three parts dry sharp sand and six parts dry aggregate. Spread the dry mix over the broken stone to a depth of about 10 cm (4 in). Make sure you have enough tiles for the job put to one side. We laid the tiles in alternate blocks of eight laid at right-angles to each other, first a block of eight across the trench, then a block laid lengthways – and so on.

3 Make up a second dry mix, this time of one part cement to three parts dry soft sand and one part dry sharp sand. Lay the tiles on edge and about 12 mm ($^1/_2$ in) apart in the dry mix already in the trench. Use the second dry mix to fill the gaps between the tiles, removing any excess mortar with the hand brush. Tap the tiles level with the handle of the trowel, using the spirit level to ensure accuracy.

4 Repeat the above two stages to lay the slates in the trench where required. The gap between the slates will be less than that used for the tiles and it will prove far simpler to lay them across the width of the trench rather than lengthways. Slates are quite fragile: if you need to tap them into the dry mix, use the handle of the trowel or the club hammer cushioned by a piece of wood.

5 When the edging is completed, check it with the spirit level. Ideally the surface of the edging should be just above that of the earth to be retained behind it and flush with any paved or other surface abutting it. While the concrete and mortar mixes are still dry, use the club hammer with a cushion of wood to gently tap the slates and tiles into their final position.

6 Cover the newly laid edging with sacks or another waterproof material to protect it from rain and leave for at least two days to take up moisture from the soil and harden. In particularly dry weather, sprinkle water over the finished edging with a watering can fitted with a fine rose. Finish by laying any paving or other surface up to the edging.

OFFCUT SLEEPERS EDGING

EQUIPMENT

Chain saw or cross-cut saw
Old paintbrush or household brush
String and pegs
Shovel
Cement-mixing board or wheelbarrow
Club hammer
Cement trowel
Spirit level

MATERIALS

Selection of railway sleeper offcuts
Spirit-based wood preservative
Quantity broken stone
Cement
Sharp builders' sand
Aggregate
Water

Safety note

It is advised that protective clothing and full face protection are worn when using a chain saw and that eye protection and rubber or protective gloves are used when applying wood preservative.

Railway sleepers have become the ubiquitous yet essential raw material for almost every television garden make-over programme or newspaper article on restoring a garden produced or written over the last few years. Invaluable for constructing 'lazy' or raised beds, for building casual steps, or for terracing a sloping garden, we have used railway sleepers for innumerable purposes within our garden and have accumulated a store of offcuts from them, too short for use or too saturated with tar for burning in an open fire.

We wanted to find a practical use for the accumulated offcuts. Some we have used on end as 'paving' in a patio and others as stepping stones in a wild area of the garden. We decided that a number of them could be usefully incorporated as one of the variety of different edging materials we planned to use in our new raised-patio herb garden.

The railway sleepers used for different parts of our garden had been secured from a variety of sources and some, particularly those salvaged from the restoration of our farming neighbour's new silage clamp, were quite rotten. We had trimmed the sleepers to size and some of the offcuts would require preservation before being used.

OFFCUT SLEEPERS EDGING

METHOD

1 Use the chain saw or cross-cut saw to cut the railway sleeper offcuts into blocks of uniform length, approximately 25 cm (10 in) long. Make sure that at least one end of each block is relatively sound and square.

2 Lay the blocks on a disposable surface. Using the old paintbrush or household brush, saturate the blocks with a spirit-based preservative, making sure in particular that the newly cut ends are covered. Leave to dry completely before continuing.

3 Mark out the proposed position of the edging with the string and pegs and dig a trench along it at least 25 cm (10 in) deep. Line the base to a depth of approximately 75 mm (3 in) with loose stone. Make a dry mixture on the mixing board or in the wheelbarrow of one part cement to three parts sharp sand and six parts aggregate. Lay this mixture in the trench to within approximately 75 mm (3 in) of the ground surface.

4 Make a further but wet mix of one part cement to four parts soft sand. Place the blocks in position on a layer of the wet mortar mix laid on the dry concrete mix approximately 12 mm ($1/2$ in) apart, leaving the tops approximately 75 to 100 mm (3 to 4 in) above ground level. Fill the gaps between the blocks with further wet mortar, smoothed to shape with the trowel. Use the string and pegs to check the alignment of the blocks and the spirit level to check that they are level, making any necessary adjustments with the club hammer or handle of the trowel.

Stone steps leading to
the fountain house in
Chrissy Price's innovative
garden. The steps were
constructed with old
paving stones that were
rescued from under
layers of bitumen.

Vita Sackville-West's White Garden at Sissinghurst Castle, in Kent, is perhaps the most famous, the most documented and the most copied themed garden. Using colour as a theme

Visit any of the major garden shows in London or elsewhere and you will find unexpected pleasure in discovering Japanese, African or Australian gardens right in the heart of

THE THEMED GARDEN

on which to base a garden design – whether it is in the hot spectrum of reds, yellows, oranges and pinks, or the cool blues, greens, purples and violets – is certain to draw the eye and make an impact, bringing colour to a garden from spring through late summer to autumn.

the city! In the subtropical atmosphere of Tresco Abbey Gardens on the Isles of Scilly (known as England's Island of Flowers) the visitor can wander at will through lines of soaring palm trees past a rocky Mexican garden to the terraces of the Mediterranean garden.

ABOVE

'In Memory of Everlasting Soles'. An unfinished garden sculpture by Paul Grellier which has used old iron shoe lasts and a salvaged churchyard plaque mounted on a stone plinth.

TOP RIGHT

The refurbished White Garden at Birtsmorton Court showing the specially commissioned lead fountain and impressive iron arches and pergolas. Reclaimed bricks and stone were used throughout this beautifully recreated garden.

BOTTOM RIGHT

A timber seat hidden in a secluded corner of Tresco Abbey gardens on the Isles of Scilly. The stone supports were rescued from the twelfth-century Abbey ruins and the posts are repaired examples of original terracotta pots.

OPPOSITE LEFT

The formality of this garden pool edged with reclaimed and mellow stone pavers is offset by the simplicity of the lawned surround and the yellow flag irises in garden designer Sarah Giddens' walled garden.

OPPOSITE CENTRE

Ancient quern stones once used to grind corn, make an interesting detail in a hidden corner of Tresco Abbey Gardens.

OPPOSITE RIGHT

The shallow, lichen covered steps leading down to this pond were made from old coping stones rescued from a demolished garden wall.

Other themes which make a strong statement are herb, rock, water and wild gardens. The last are important natural habitats for birds, animals and insect life and if they include woodlands can be home to masses of wild flowers and lush ferns. Take it one step further and a woodland garden can become a jungle, overflowing with palms, giant gunnera, bamboo thickets and numerous exotic trees, shrubs and marsh plants, as in the Jungle Garden at the Lost Gardens of Heligan in Cornwall.

Moving from natural wilderness to more formal gardens, props can be used to great effect as decoration. Place statuary stone lions, dogs and deer alongside ornate urns and vessels on plinths to create a 'gallery', adding a touch of grandeur to even the most modest of outdoor rooms.

Containers provide an instant effect, whether they are wooden tubs on a terrace or terracotta pots on a patio. Metal tubs, dustbins and old galvanised florists' buckets look particularly striking when planted with clipped trees or topiary shrubs and silvery foliage. If this somewhat contrived look is not to everyone's taste, old-fashioned metal buckets can be planted with a variety of plants for a more informal appearance. Enjoy the richly aromatic fragrances of herbs in the warmth of sunlight by planting rosemary, thyme, parsley, sage, chives, marjoram, bay, basil, coriander and mint in buckets outside the back door.

The sensuous sounds of water in the garden trickling, rushing, gushing and cascading, bring about a feeling of calm, soothing away the tension and anxiety that builds up in our daily lives. Electricity which we take so much for granted allows power to be taken to the most far-flung parts of the garden for artificial waterfalls and fountains. A rectangular, square or circular pool which may be home to koi carp or goldfish can be quite a formal feature, whereas a wildlife pond, a home for flora and fauna such as water lilies, dragonflies, frogs and toads, has a more informal, natural appearance.

Whichever theme or combination of themes is chosen for a garden, wood will play its part. Contrasting superbly with natural foliage and materials like stone, slate, brick and terracotta, it can be used in many ways both structurally and decoratively. Create boundaries with attractive picket fencing made from redundant pallets, or transform railway sleepers into sweeping steps leading to borders flanked by heavenly scented lavender bushes, or a froth of Alchemilla mollis, to soften the hard edges. In kitchen gardens, railway sleepers make hugely practical lazy beds containing succulent beans, courgettes and spinach.

Teak is a hardwood that is very popular for garden furniture as it is long lasting and fades to a glorious grey colour. A softwood hexagonal table which we found in a garden nursery and was once used to display stock has been reborn in a buttercup meadow, its surface planted with turf in readiness for a summer picnic, where it looks romantically ephemeral and wonderfully surreal!

WATER FEATURE

EQUIPMENT

Wire brush
Paint brush
Face mask
Spirit level

MATERIALS

Old steel cattle trough (or other suitable
    water tank)
Bitumen paint (check it is safe for
    pond use)
Red oxide metal primer paint
Spray can of multi-surface outdoor paint
Electric fountain (or water pump)

Safety note

Electricity is extremely dangerous, especially if
used in or close to water. Only use safety-checked
equipment specifically manufactured for outdoor
and underwater use and get expert advice before
connecting it to mains power. Special outdoor
fittings and wiring are essential for outdoor use or
damp conditions. Electric shocks received from
incorrectly fitted or inappropriate equipment,
particularly when used in the presence of water,
can cause serious injury or even kill, so don't take
chances: seek advice from a qualified electrician.

A great deal has been written
about water features in gardens,
with good reason. Running water
adds the dimensions of sound
and movement to a garden, and
the presence of water – whether
running or still – will enrich the
wildlife in a garden, attracting to
it numerous birds, animals and
insects requiring a year-round
supply of drinking water.

Water can give a focal point to
a garden as well as offering the
opportunity to grow a whole new
range of plants. Whatever your
choice of water feature, it is well
worth reading up on the subject
and consulting a local expert
retailer about the various marginal
and other suitable plants you can
use and which, if any, fish to
stock it with. As fish need oxygen
to survive, it is most important
that the feature is planted with
oxygenating plants or some
mechanical means is used to
keep the oxygen level of the water
at the correct balance.

Farmers often stock the
cattle troughs in their fields with
goldfish, perhaps won at the
annual village fair, but they serve
a useful function in helping to
keep the troughs clean of insect
larvae and other impurities. Our
old but serviceable cattle trough,
purchased at a farm sale, was
incorporated into our paved
garden using a small and
inexpensive fountain to aerate
the water and provide the
attractions of sound and
movement.

WATER FEATURE

METHOD

When choosing a trough or tank for this project make sure that the steel is sound, without holes or perforations. Troughs which have a hole or fitting near the top for the old water supply are ideal as the hole will provide a concealed access for the fountain's power cable.

1 Scrub the trough vigorously with a stiff wire brush to remove any rust or loose and flaking material. Clean the trough both inside and out, paying particular attention to the base which might be in contact with the ground when installed and therefore especially prone to rust.

2 Turn the trough onto its side and brush out any remaining loose material or rust debris. Apply two coats of black bitumen paint to the inside of the trough up to the level of any access hole or, if none exists, to within approximately 5 cm (2 in) of the top. Make sure the entire surface is well covered. Leave to dry.

3 Apply a coat of red oxide metal primer paint to those parts of the trough, inside and out, not covered by the bitumen paint. Leave to dry completely, then apply a second coat and leave to dry.

4 Apply one or two finishing coats of multi-surface outdoor paint over the red oxide primer. We chose to use a purpose-made spray paint to give an even finish, but similar paints can be applied by brush. Always use a face mask if spray painting and follow the manufacturer's recommendations on the tin.

5 Install the painted trough in position. Once it is filled with water it will be extremely heavy so make sure it is exactly where you want it to be, checking its alignment with a spirit level. (We chose to raise our trough onto four bricks rather than have it sitting on the ground which can encourage rust.) Fill the trough with water to the top of the bitumen, ideally using rainwater though tap water can be used.

6 Read thoroughly the installation instructions which accompany the fountain. Feed its electric cable through the trough's access hole, if one exists, or pass it over the top of the tank into the water and place the fountain in position. It may be necessary to raise the fountain onto stones or bricks so that it is at the correct level in the water. If desired you can drill a hole into the tank just above the water level to take the electrical supply and seal the hole with waterproof mastic. Please see the safety note on page 190. It is most important that the equipment and the power supply is checked before the power is turned on. Once this is done, plant your trough with water plants, turn on the fountain and enjoy the ambiance that trickling water creates.

Please read the important safety note on page 190: it is most important that the equipment and the power supply is checked before the power is turned on. Once this is done, plant your trough with water plants, turn on the fountain and enjoy the ambiance that trickling water creates.

METAL BUCKET PLANTING

EQUIPMENT

Electric drill and 6 mm (¹/₄ in) metal drill bit
Paintbrush (optional)

MATERIALS

Old metal bucket
Black bitumen paint (optional)
Metal lacquer (optional)
Selection of stones or broken
    terracotta pots

METHOD

1 If the bucket being used as a planter has no perforations in its base, drill a number of holes to provide drainage to prevent the soil becoming saturated and the plants overwatered.

2 If desired, paint the inside of the bucket with black butumen paint and the outside with a coat of protective metal lacquer to preserve the appearance of the metal and help prevent further corrosion. Fill the bottom 5 to 10 cm (2 to 4 in) of the bucket with broken pot shards or stones to allow free drainage to the drilled holes in the base. Add soil or planting mixture and place your selected plant in position, firming the soil around it.

Zinc and other metal planters and containers are enjoying a resurgence in popularity in garden fashion. Our commitment to the reuse of old materials has led to the making of planters from old bread tins and dustbins, garden edging from corrugated-iron strips, arbours from metal reinforcement rods, and numerous garden arches from offcuts of steel concrete-reinforcement sheets.

Planters created from rusty, old, battered and sometimes perforated metal buckets can be far cheaper than modern metal containers, and very effective they look too. Old or discarded buckets, when grouped together and well planted, make an attractive display on wide steps or a patio.

Many of the buckets we have used had rusted to such an extent that no drainage holes were necessary. Should this not be the case, it is important to perforate the base to provide adequate drainage.

GRASS TOP TABLE

EQUIPMENT

Old paintbrush for preservative
Pliers, wire cutters or heavy-duty scissors
Staple gun and staples
Sharp knife or craft knife
Garden sieve (optional)

MATERIALS

Old slatted wooden table
Timber preservative
Wire netting
Plastic sheeting
Quantity garden turf
Quantity sieved soil (optional)

METHOD

Any slatted table can be used for this project. Alternatively, a solid table would do if perforated with sufficient holes to provide adequate drainage. If the table selected has no retaining surround, construct one out of preservative-treated softwood timber, fixed to the edge of the table to provide a rebate of at least 10 cm (4 in).

1 Treat the whole of the table with a timber preservative, paying particular attention to end-grain timber, the legs where they will be in contact with the ground, and the table top and surround into which the soil and turf will be placed.

2 When the preservative is completely dry, cut the wire netting with the pliers, wire cutters or heavy-duty scissors to the shape of the table top and fix it in place with the staple gun.

3 Cut the plastic sheeting (we used an old tarpaulin) to fit the table top and perforate it for drainage. If the rebate is sufficiently deep, spread a layer of approximately 10 cm (4 in) of sieved soil over the entire surface. Lay the turfs on the soil or plastic liner, cut them to shape with the knife, and press firmly into place making sure the joints between the turfs are tight to allow for shrinkage. Water the feature thoroughly and keep it moist otherwise the turf will dry out. In autumn, spring bulbs can be planted between the turf and the underlying soil to provide a stunning spring flower display.

Every so often you come across something which you know is just too good to miss! Such was the case with this wooden plant display table which was bought 'for a song' as the first lot in the closing down sale of a garden nursery. Once home, the table sat outside, adding to the detritus of what has become our very own reclamation yard. We knew that one day we would find a use for it.

Events have a way of precipitating action. Early one morning, we awoke to the sound of what we thought was thunder until, looking out of the window, we saw a herd of cattle gambolling like overgrown lambs on our lawn. After five months of being penned in during winter, smelling the lush green grass of our precious lawn, they had broken out and proceeded to turn the lawn into what looked like a tank training ground or the aftermath of a pop festival.

After several weeks and a few visits from grim-faced insurance assessors, the turfing contractors came to re-lay the lawn. One week later we had a new expanse of bowling-green quality lawn and several turfs left over from the job. Inspiration struck. Why not plant our table with turf and create a year-round feature, even if as a table it would be somewhat impractical?

We planted the turfs straight into the existing shallow rebate of the table. For a lasting effect, the turf should be laid onto a base of compacted soil at least 10 cm (4 in) deep.

A stone balustrade, salvaged from a once grand, but since dilapidated house on the mainland. It is now installed in the new Mediterranean garden, one of the themed areas within the Abbey Gardens on the island of Tresco.

ELEMENTS AND AMBIANCE

Long ago, the elements were thought to be earth, water, air and fire. Here, the elements are the structures, textures, colours, planting, props and light that help to create an ambiance topiary established. Lakes and follies were designed to blend into the part-constructed countryside, interrupted only by a hidden ha-ha. Today few of us can change the physical and make a garden personal.

The great landscape designers of the past created amazing vistas by altering the natural landscape to fit an invented plan or scheme. Tree planting was undertaken on a massive scale, formal structures with large sweeps of manicured, terraced and walled gardens were formed, and parterres and characteristics of our gardens. We have to live with and work around what is already there, usually on a minute scale compared with the great estates. With monotonous regularity we clip the hedges, mow the lawns to perfection, weed the borders, and deadhead the roses in an effort to achieve a neat, tidy and well-managed garden.

ABOVE

Water pours from an old brass faucet into a reclaimed stone trough in Chrissy Price's water garden.

RIGHT

Massive stone pillars support timbers cut from storm blown trees felled during the great storm of 1990 which destroyed so much of Tresco Abbey Gardens, make an oversized pergola supporting long established kiwi fruits and passion flowers.

There is a body of people who have become bored with rows of box balls, who are reacting against symmetry, who no longer want to force flowers and plants to grow in conditions which are the very opposite of their natural habitat; who, in short, feel we should all stop fighting nature and, instead, work with it. These same people find the smoke, petrol fumes and noise pollution of the lawn mower antisocial and consider that conventional gardening involves too much destruction of the natural environment. This movement favours a looser style of lush planting for the twenty-first century, accidental-looking drifts or expanses of shape, colour and texture. Emulating nature, they advocate mixes of grasses, perennials, herbs, self-seeding annuals, even fruits grown at random, spontaneous mixes of wildflower meadows and prairies emerging under the title of 'new perennial planting'. Of course, nothing is ever quite that easy. This style of planting requires skill to make it look as if it has just happened, and it needs a degree of control, otherwise it looks a mess. But the timing is right for it; it is part of the organic, environmentally friendly trend we feel comfortable with.

LEFT

View from the stone bridge across the moat of thirteenth-century Birtsmorton Court to an entrance to the walled garden. The wrought iron gates, lead planter and staddle stones were installed during restoration work on the property.

BELOW LEFT

Old stone slabs salvaged from a farmhouse are surrounded by ancient cobbles and then bordered with an edging of reclaimed clay roof tiles to make a path through this Kiwi-fruit-shaded pergola.

BELOW RIGHT

An informal pond – a haven for wildlife – has been bridged by an old railway sleeper, entirely in keeping with the mood and colours of this part of an exciting garden.

Hankering after the flower-filled fields and meadows of our childhood, so much of it now swallowed up for development, may sound fine to those who have the rolling acres, but what about the rest of us? Do not despair – there is no reason why a scaled-down wildlife reserve cannot be planted in a back yard or clumps of graceful grasses freely cultivated on a balcony or even in a window box.

This freedom of expression is at odds with those designers who fill show gardens with bold concepts in concrete, metal and glass with only the occasional nod towards the token plant. If you find this controlled style both ugly and brutal, look to where your pleasure lies.

Perhaps you have a fleeting image of an evolving space whose structures are a succession of mellow brickwork walls, gentrified cobbles, gnarled and knobbly wooden fences, glorious slate terraces in greys, blues, blacks and heathers; summer houses laced with an air of mystery, their ancient windows of uneven glass and pathways of muddy brown stone and shingle. Linked by a natural theme of scents from flowers and herbs, sounds from birds and insects with the distant gurgle of water, it is a haven of refuge offering a kind of spiritualism which seems to be missing in many of our daily lives.

GLOVE STAND

EQUIPMENT

Craft knife
Electric drill
Selection of spade bits

MATERIALS

Selection of firewood offcuts
Glasspaper
Waterproof wood glue

METHOD

Choose the timber you will use for this project carefully, ensuring it is dry and well seasoned. You will need to select a larger heavy piece with one flat surface for the base and a number of fairly thin, similarly sized straight branches for the uprights.

1 Use the craft knife and glasspaper to remove any bark from the timber and sand to a smooth finish. Cut the branches to an equal length to form the uprights. Round off the top or smaller end of each upright with glasspaper.

2 Trim the bottom or larger end of each upright with the craft knife and glasspaper into a uniform tapered shape.

3 Using the drill and spade bit, cut a hole for each upright in the base piece. Drill each hole at a slight angle from the vertical so that when the uprights are fitted into place they will splay at a consistent angle.

4 Apply waterproof wood glue to each hole and fit the uprights firmly into position. Check the splay and put the completed stand to one side to dry. You might wish to finish the stand with an application of wood perservative or furniture wax.

What to do with the perishable rubber gloves used for outdoor painting when they are not in use? Where to keep the leather pruning gauntlets when they are damp? And anyway, where are they? However neat the garden room or potting shed, the multitude of gloves needed for the various jobs round the garden have a habit of getting mislaid or obdurately secreting themselves in some dark and dusty corner.

In an attempt to tackle this problem, we have come up with a storage stand for the many different garden gloves that we all seem to own. A simple stand which will store damp gloves allowing them to dry properly, an object both functional and pleasing to look at.

The view from the Somerset farmhouse where we used to live was over a Site of Special Scientific Interest and a European Heritage Area. In other words we lived in an area where English Nature and the Department for the Environment, Farming and Rural Affairs closely control the management of the countryside. Willow trees (locally known as 'withies') line every rhine and ditch and farmers must pollard them (known as 'shading') on a regular basis. As well as delighting in a constantly changing landscape, we therefore enjoyed an abundance of offcut wood, the perfect resource for our project.

GARDEN LIGHT

EQUIPMENT

Orbital sander or glasspaper
Tape measure
Hand saw
Electric drill and wood drill bits
Electric (or hand) screwdriver
Pencil or marker pen
Straight edge
Paintbrush

MATERIALS

Wooden framed stained-glass window
Glazing putty (if necessary)
Length 25 mm (1 in) square timber (battens)
Quantity 50 mm (2 in) wood screws
Length 20 cm (8 in) x 25 mm (1 in) planed
    timber (sides and base)
Multi-surface outdoor paint

When daylight has dwindled, night-time dining outdoors by the soft light of candles is particularly pleasurable. A bewildering selection of electrical outdoor lights can be purchased but we prefer the glow from lamps and the flickering light of flares. For different occasions we have glass candle lights on tall metal spikes that we insert in the grass and borders, nightlights in antique Victorian glass containers, and others in small faceted tumblers. We own several old paraffin lamps bought at farm auctions and have made numerous candle holders from old farm and garden tools, staircase spindles and clay ink bottles found at car-boot sales.

When asking reclamation dealers what they find difficult to sell, one answer is the small stained-glass windows removed from late-nineteenth and early-twentieth century houses, for which there seems to be little alternative use. Easy to find and inexpensive to buy, we thought they could be simply converted into garden lights which, standing on a low wall or table, cast an attractive diffused glow through their patterned glass. We have made many of these lights and others have been used to cover recessed wall lights. One we have inserted into the gable end of a garden shed to cast patterned shafts of coloured light onto an otherwise boring interior.

GARDEN LIGHT

METHOD

1 Use the orbital sander or glasspaper to remove any loose or flaking paint from the window frame. It is not essential to remove all the paint but important to provide a sound surface for subsequent painting. Make good any putty missing from the front of the window.

2 Turn the frame onto its front, the back uppermost, and measure its height. Cut the 25 mm (1 in) square timber into two battens, each approximately 4 cm (1½ in) less than the height of the frame. Pre-drill screw holes along the length of each batten and attach to the rear of the frame 25 mm (1 in) from each outside edge with 50 mm (2 in) screws. (The distance the battens are fitted inside the edges of the frame will depend on the thickness of timber you are using for the sides. Measure your timber and adjust this dimension accordingly.) The battens should be attached approximately 25 mm (1 in) from the bottom and 15 mm (½ in) from the top of the frame.

3 Place the 20 cm (8 in) x 25 mm (1 in) planed timber on the work surface and make sure its end is square. (If you are using timber such as an old floorboard, you will probably need to cut the end off in order to discard damaged wood.) Mark a point the distance of the height of the frame along one edge of the plank. Mark a second point approximately 25 mm (1 in) less on the opposite edge of the plank. Join the points with a pencil or marker pen and straight edge and saw along the line. Using this sloping cut end as a pattern, cut a second identical piece from the remainder of the plank.

4 Place one of the cut sides onto the back of the frame and butted against the batten with the sloping end towards the top and the taller edge to the front. Pre-drill screw holes and fix to the batten with at least three 50 mm (2 in) wood screws, making sure not to insert any screw within 25 mm (1 in) of the bottom. Repeat with the other side piece.

5 Measure the distance between the side pieces assembled on the frame and cut another piece of the 20 cm (8 in) x 25 mm (1 in) planed timber to that measurement to form the base. Attach the base to the frame using 50 mm (2 in) wood screws driven through pre-drilled holes in the side pieces. Your assembled sloping-sided light should now be able to stand in position without additional support.

6 Paint all the wood surfaces with multi-surface garden paint, place a candle inside a secure metal or other fire-resistant container behind the stained glass, and the garden light is ready to use.

SLATE BOARD

EQUIPMENT

Slate cutter
Palette knife or paint scraper
Selection of different grades
  glasspaper or emery paper
Electric drill and 6 mm ($^1/_4$ in) bit
Block of scrap wood
Paintbrush (optional)

MATERIALS

Selection old roofing slates
20 cm (8 in) length of leather
  bootlace for each slate
Matt or satin finish exterior-grade
  varnish (optional)

METHOD

1 The size of the slate board will depend on the slate available but this is a very useful way of using smaller or broken slates. Slates are normally hand split and cut to create one bevelled edge and one flat edge. The slate cutter is designed to produce a similar cut edge and we recommend you experiment with it on scrap slate to familiarise yourself with how it cuts before cutting your project slates to size.

2 Use the paint scraper or palette knife to remove any flaking or delamination to reveal the sound surface underneath. Use glasspaper or emery paper to sand the slate smooth, starting with course grade and finishing with fine grade paper to achieve the best finish. Place the slate on a piece of waste timber and with the electric drill and 6 mm ($^1/_4$ in) bit drill a hole through from the top (i.e. the side with the bevelled edge), centred about 25 mm (1 in) from the top of the slate. Drilling through the slate into scrap timber will minimise any risk of the slate breaking while the hole is being cut.

3 Feed the leather bootlace or strips cut from scrap leather through the hole, tie into a simple knot and the slate board is ready for hanging from a hook or nail, the perfect aide-mémoire for the garden room or potting shed. If desired, the slate surface can be sealed with a coat of matt or satin exterior-grade varnish.

Slate is lovely to look at, has an interesting texture, and is one of the most versatile of salvaged materials with a multiplicity of uses throughout the home and garden. We show how salvaged slate can be used to make garden markers (page 224) and edging (page 178), and in the chapter 'A Garden Reclaimed' we illustrate how broken and chipped slate, collected from slate cutting at a reclamation yard, can be used as a very effective and attractive garden mulch. Old slates can be used to isolate invasive plants such as mint in a herb bed and as tiles on the surface of a stone or wooden table. The offcuts from thick slate which has been cut down to make flooring slabs and kitchen work surfaces can be obtained from flooring contractors to make an imposing path edge.

Reclaimed roof slates are easily cut and even when heavily delaminated or flaking through exposure to air, rain and weather, can be simply converted into invaluable place mats, memo boards and clipboards for the home and garden. In this project we show how to make a stylish slate memo board but the project can be easily adapted to create a clipboard by fitting a bulldog clip to the top to hold a paper pad.

When writing with chalk on a slate board, wet the chalk first. This simple hint will ensure that your writing stands out effectively when the chalk has dried.

TOOL RACK

EQUIPMENT

Tape measure
Carpenter's square
Pencil
Hand saw
Straight edge
Jig saw (optional)
Electric drill
38 mm (1¹/₂ in) hole cutter bit
25 mm (1 in) wood chisel
Wood drill bits to fit screws
Electric (or hand) screwdriver

MATERIALS

Selection timber:
2 pieces approx. 40 cm (16 in) x 90 cm
    (36 in) x 25 mm (1 in) (sides)
2 pieces approx 25cm (10 in) x 110 cm
    (43 in) x 25 mm (1 in) (top and base)
1 piece approx 15 cm (6 in) x 110cm (43 in)
    x 25 mm (1 in) (rear)
Selection approx 65 mm (2¹/₂ in) screws

METHOD

1 Take the two pieces of 25 cm (10 in) x 90 cm (36 in) x 25 mm (1 in) timber and mark two lines approximately 5 cm (2 in) inside from each edge with the pencil and straight edge along the length of one face of each piece. Starting 5 cm (2 in) from one end, mark points at 20 cm (8 in) intervals on each line to give two rows of five marks. Select one board as the top and drill holes through at the marked points with the electric drill and hole cutter. On the second board which will form the base, drill holes with the hole cutter at the marked points but only to a depth of approximately 12 mm (¹/₂ in). Remove the cut wood with the wood chisel to give a rebated hole into which the tool handles will eventually sit.

2 Mark a point 25 cm (10 in) on one face at one end of each of the two pieces of 40 cm (16 in) x 90 cm (36 in) x 25 mm (1 in) timber and with the pencil and straight edge draw a line from these points to the full 40 cm (16 in) width of the timber at the opposite end. Use the hand saw or jig saw to cut along the drawn lines to make the two sides measuring 90 cm (36 in) x 40 cm (16 in) (base) and 25 cm (10 in) (top).

3 Measure a point 5 cm (2 in) from the base of both side pieces and use the carpenters square and straight edge to draw a line across each piece. Fit the top piece of drilled 25 cm (10 in) x 110 cm (43 in) x 25 mm (1 in) timber inside and flush with the 25 cm (10 in) end of both cut side pieces with screws. Pre-drill screwholes before assembling to prevent the timber splitting. Fit the base piece of 25 cm (10 in) x 110 cm (43 in) x 25 mm (1 in) timber, with the half drilled holes facing up and inside the 40 cm (16 in) ends of the side pieces at the line drawn 5 cm (2 in) up from the base so that the base will be raised 5 cm (2 in) off the ground when the rack is placed in position.

4 To reinforce the structure and stop the construction 'racking', screw the 15 cm (6 in) x 110 cm (43 in) x 25 mm (1 in) rear piece inside the back of the tool rack so that it fits under the top piece. Tighten all screws to secure the construction, place on a flat surface and the tool rack is ready for use.

Two things with irresistible appeal for us are interesting old tools and reclaimed timber. Finds from sources ranging from skips to garage sales have included some superb lengths of figured antique elm which now form the head and foot boards of a four poster bed, massive moulded cornices which when stripped of layers of white paint were revealed to be carved from solid oak, and large quantities of both painted and unpainted softwood which we have used for numerous projects saving considerable expenditure on new wood. We have a store stacked from floor to ceiling with reclaimed timber and some of this was used to construct the tool rack.

Garden tool storage is a constant problem. Our accumulation of old and modern tools and garden equipment makes a considerable inroad into already limited space and although we have fitted a tool shed with a peg board round the walls from which to hang many of the tools, some inevitably end up in a corner of the room. To store some of our numerous straight-handled tools, we decided to construct a simple free-standing rack to keep them in order. The project shows how a modestly sized rack can be constructed but the design can of course be adjusted to be larger or smaller to suit your own particular needs.

TRELLIS WALL RACK

EQUIPMENT

Pencil
Spirit level
Hand saw
Electric drill
Wood drill bit (to fit screws)
Bradawl
Masonry bit (for solid walls)
Screwdriver

MATERIALS

Old trellis
Two lengths waste timber batten
Selection wall plugs (for solid walls)
Selection screws
Metal cup hooks

METHOD

1 Place the trellis against the wall in the selected position with the horizontal bars facing out and mark on the wall the positions of the second bar from the top and the second bar from the bottom, checking the alignment with the spirit level. Cut two lengths of batten to the width of the trellis. Using the electric drill and wood bit, drill fixing holes in the battens approximately 20 cm (8 in) from each end. Align the top batten with the positional marks on the wall, mark the position of the fixing holes on the wall using the bradawl, then repeat for the bottom batten. Drill holes into the wall with the electric drill and masonry bit, fill the holes with wall plugs, and screw the battens to the wall.

2 Using the wood bit, drill fixing holes through two thicknesses of trellis where the vertical bars cross the second horizontal bar from the top and bottom. Offer the trellis up against the wall so that the battens are hidden by the horizontal bars of the trellis. Secure in place with screws driven through the fixing holes into the battens behind, using the spirit level to check for accuracy. Fit cup hooks to the horizontal bars as required.

As the plans for our garden change or evolve, we are often left with redundant trellis. Much we cut down or adapt for a different location but, when we decided to refurnish our garden room, we reserved one piece as a wall storage rack on which to keep all those notes, packets of seed and other miscellanea which would otherwise create clutter.

Nothing could be simpler, yet – properly secured to a wall – a trellis rack is an invaluable addition to a practical work area or potting shed. We have also used old trellis fixed to the ceiling of a tool store. Using metal 'S' hooks, we hang from it such things as garden umbrellas over winter, terracotta wall pots to protect them from the frost, string bags of bulbs awaiting planting, and even bunches of flowers left to dry.

Although garden trellis is readily available and inexpensive, we dislike the colours commercially available trellis is stained. We prefer to make most of our own from offcut softwood waste timber, protecting it with outdoor preservative stained with various pigments to achieve a subdued shade to merge with the background against which the trellis is erected.

Stunning Fountain' built
y sculptor Paul Grellier
nd constructed of
eclaimed stone and an
ld post-hole auger.

Before disposing of items or relics that appear to be past their useful life, exercise a little lateral thinking as almost anything can be reused.

Over the past twenty-five years

INVENTIVE IDEAS

we have greatly increased our consumption of wine which means the task of recycling our empty wine bottles is done with a sense of duty rather than enthusiasm. Having downed the last drop of Chardonnay, the empty container gets slung onto a mounting pile before being transported to the local bottle bank, from where it is collected for recycling. We visited a garden where empty bottles had been saved and used to create a garden feature. Rows of neatly arranged green wine bottles were stacked from floor to ceiling in the alcove of a high, old stone wall. With sunlight bouncing off their bases, this exciting creation resembled a huge honeycomb.

Empty wine bottles can also be used to make idiosyncratic garden sculptures, their necks wedged randomly into the stump of a decaying tree. Colourful recycled glass chippings, purchased from garden supply stores can be used to great effect to create paths, make a mulch or in a water feature.

NEAR RIGHT

A mirror, framed by a mosaic of pebbles, stones and broken coloured china in garden designer Sue Berger's town centre garden, leads the visitor towards an imaginary doorway into another secret garden.

CENTRE LEFT

A scarecrow constructed mainly of old clay flower pots with flowering chives growing from its head. A light-hearted flight of fancy in the garden of Emmaüs House, a retreat and conference centre.

CENTRE RIGHT

Weathered coping stones laid in a broken line and overgrown with a profusion of verdant plants in a wild flower bed at Emmaus House give the appearance of a fallen and half-buried stone column.

FAR RIGHT

This galvanised steel bird table was made from a variety of rescued components by an enthusiast who spends much of his leisure time scavenging for the raw materials for his imaginative constructions.

BOTTOM LEFT

This ancient oak gate post, complete with its original iron latch stop has been left in position in the garden of a village house to make an unusual feature.

BOTTOM RIGHT

Empty wine bottles from the restaurant at Emmaüs House stacked from floor to ceiling in a garden wall alcove make an eye-catching feature when illuminated by the sun.

Another garden we visited was stuffed with practical and inventive recycling ideas. It sported wine corks on spikes to support fruit netting without causing damage to the net, or indeed a poke in the eye; telephone wires fixed against the walls for training roses and other climbers; large terracotta pots turned upside down and topped with wooden slats to form a potting surface; and even a horse's saddle rest attached to an outside wall housing a garden hose. (The hose reel in this chapter was made from an abandoned electric cable drum.) An old window frame, complete with glass, was put to good use as the lid on a cold frame and generous-sized garden markers were cut from salvaged timber and roofing slate.

On an agricultural note, old farm equipment can be put to good use in gardens. Stable hay feeders make good planters for a colourful flower display and old harrows can be fixed to a wall and used as supports for climbing plants. A retired farmer used timber from a disused calf pen and salvaged telegraph poles to make a pool-side bench and table, while the cart shafts featured in this chapter were decoratively installed to emphasise a view. Even the peeling white painted wall within a linhay has been cleverly adorned with a collection of salvaged artefacts, including rusty tools, a battered wooden shelf, assorted implements, ancient horseshoes and an antlered skull!

Less unusual but not to be dismissed are cast-iron gutter hoppers which can be fixed to a wall or cartwheel and planted with summer blooms. Likewise, old clay roof hip tiles and flowerpots attached to ridge tiles and filled with colourful flowers provide a vibrant display from spring through to autumn. A simple oak whisky barrel cut in half and planted is another sight seen almost everywhere.

The average garden may not have room for a gargantuan stone fallen 'column', cleverly contrived from salvaged coping stones, creating an informal moss-covered border lying strewn on the earth like some prehistoric reptile. We came across just this in Emmaüs House, a conference centre and retreat run by nuns. In the same garden we turned a corner and to our surprise encountered the figure of a man, made entirely out of old flowerpots, sitting with hoe in hand and chives for hair – a bit of light-hearted fun to frighten off the birds!

Mirrors used on a garden wall are a clever trick when attempting to make a space seem larger, which is particularly useful in small town gardens. An artist friend attached a bamboo-framed mirror, painted soft lavender blue, to a patio wall and allowed ivy and other creepers to spread and drape themselves around it. They blended so well with the frame that the mirror was at first glance disguised, giving the illusion of light in an enlarged area. Garden designer Susan Berger created a handsome Gothic arch from stones, pebbles, shells and broken china on the ivy-clad wall of her metropolitan garden, fooling the visitor into believing that it leads to another secret enclosure. She also welded together old steel reinforcement rods (usually used to support concrete frame buildings) to form a rusty, barley-twist pergola which in the height of summer is covered in roses, clematis and a rampant golden leaf vine.

HOSE REEL

EQUIPMENT

Hand saw
Electric or hand screwdriver
Electric jigsaw
Electric orbital sander or glasspaper
Paintbrush

MATERIALS

Empty plywood cable drum
Selection tongue-and-groove cladding
Selection 20 mm ($^3/_4$ in) wood screws
Multi-surface garden paint
Four 60 mm ($2^1/_2$ in) wood screws

A garden hose is essential in any well managed garden, but its storage can be a nightmare. Hoses seem to have a life of their own. Wound up in a coil, they always seem to develop tangles; when unwound, the flow of water is prevented by mysteriously appearing kinks and bends. To prolong the life of a hose and prevent accidental damage, it should always be housed on a reel when not in use. Hose reels are readily available from shops and garden centres and most do a good job – but at a cost. Here we show how an effective wall-mounted hose reel can be simply constructed from a discarded cable drum with only basic tools and a little patience.

Cable drums come in many sizes, from gigantic wooden drums unreeled from the back of a cable-laying vehicle to cardboard drums on which domestic electric cable is sold. Most larger drums are recycled, returned to the cable manufacture for reuse, but if you can secure one it can be transformed into a practical garden table. For this hose-reel project, we used a plywood electric-cable drum which we found abandoned on an industrial building site, a source of numerous useful finds.

HOSE REEL

METHOD

1 Saw the tongue-and-groove cladding into lengths roughly the diameter of the cable drum, join the boards together and lay them face down on the work surface. Lay the drum on top and fix it to the tongue-and-groove, using two 18 mm ($^3/_4$ in) wood screws to secure each board.

2 Place the drum and fitted boards onto a block of wood raised above the work surface and cut the boards to shape with the jigsaw, using the circular drum base as a guide.

3 Turn the drum over and use the orbital sander or glasspaper to give a smooth and rounded finish to the newly cut edge.

4 Apply at least two coats of multi-surface garden paint of your chosen colour to the whole of the hose reel, remembering to paint the rear to protect it from water and decay.

5 When the paint is dry, the hose reel can be secured in position with the four 60 mm ($2^1/_2$ in) wood screws driven through its base into the wall behind. (If secured to a solid wall, the screws should be driven into wall plugs inserted into previously made holes drilled with a masonry bit.) Touch up exposed screw heads with a dab of paint. The reel is now ready for use.

CLAY PIPE PLANTERS

EQUIPMENT

Garden spade
Garden trowel

MATERIALS

Selection clay drainage pipes
Sieved soil, compost or
   growing medium

METHOD

1 Decide where the pipes are to be positioned then dig a trench slightly deeper than the depth you propose to sink the deepest pipe. Place a layer of stone or broken potshards in the base of the trench to provide a firm footing for the pipes.

2 Place the deepest pipe into position and then add the others, supporting their bases by building up the foundation of stone and broken pots under them. Fill around the base of each pipe with soil, firming into place to secure it properly.

3 Fill the pipes with growing mixture, compost or sieved soil, leaving a bit of space between the soil and the top of the pipes in order to make watering easier. Water thoroughly and plant. It can be quite difficult to control the growth of weeds around grouped pipe planters, so it is worth mulching around their bases.

Terracotta drainage and soil pipes are readily available and can be found in numerous lengths, guages and finishes. Some are now being replaced with plastic but the traditional clay pipe is still widely used.

Many clay pipes would seem to be broken either in transit or during installation and damaged ones are a familar sight around most building developments. Broken pipes are of little or no use to the builder or contractor and they can often be rescued before they are broken up to make hardcore, their otherwise inevitable end.

Clay pipes can be used to construct effective garden features. Pipes inserted into the ground at different depths, or a combination of pipes of varying lengths, add height, texture and an almost architectural quality to a garden, border or bed. The fact that most pipes are made with one flush and one ferruled end offers further opportunities to vary the appearance of a feature.

Short lengths of pipe can be most attractive when used as containers inserted into the soil to control the otherwise rampant growth of certain invasive plants. They can also be most attractive when installed flush with the surface of paved areas to contain low-growing herbs or sweet-smelling plants.

GARDEN MARKERS

Serried ranks of twigs and sticks surmounted by tatty seed packets placed in the garden to identify rows of seedlings or emerging plants can be a bit of an eyesore.

Slugs attack most of the packets, the writing fades and becomes illegible, and anyway, half go missing, blown or washed away. Plastic markers do an excellent job and can be used to mark repotted plants or cuttings to record species and dates, but the gardener with an eye to combining practicality and aesthetics will always find a use for robust and attractive garden markers which are easily read and can be used time and time again.

Slate is an obvious choice of material for making garden markers: strong and almost impervious to decay or degradation, its colour is perfect for writing on in chalk or white paint. We demonstrate how to transform redundant roofing slates into simple and long-lasting garden markers.

Wood is another excellent material from which to make garden markers and we show how softwood timber rescued from a broken picket fence can be transformed into highly individual markers. Almost any wood can be utilised and should you have access to a ripsaw or saw bench, it is simple to cut down waste softwood or hardwood timber to a suitable size.

SLATE MARKERS

EQUIPMENT

Tape measure
Straight edge
Marker point or nail
Slate cutter
Palette knife or paint scraper
Electric orbital sander
    (or various grades of glasspaper
    and emery paper)
Paintbrush

MATERIALS

Selection roofing slates
Matt or satin finish
    exterior-grade varnish

METHOD

All slate has a grain and roofing slates are generally cut with the grain running along the length of the slate. A slate cutter will make a better job cutting across the grain. This project requires the markers to be cut into strips along the grain, so particular care should be taken.

1 Use the tape measure, straight edge and marker point or nail to divide the width of the slate into strips approximately 6 cm (2$^1/_4$ in) wide. Cut the strips with the slate cutter. As the action of the slate cutter will produce one bevelled edge and one flat edge, always cut the slate from the same face in order to produce a matching cut.

2 Cut each strip of slate to the desired length and create a point at one end by cutting from both edges at an angle of approximately 45°. This can be quite tricky and may result in a number of broken points before you master the technique. (Keep pieces of broken and chipped slate for use as a garden bedding mulch.)

3 Lay the completed markers on a flat surface and remove any delamination or flaked material with the palette knife or scraper. Use the orbital sander (or varying grades of glasspaper and emery paper) to sand to a smooth finish.

4 Wipe clean of any dust and debris and apply two coats of matt or satin outdoor varnish with the paintbrush, leaving to dry between coats. When the second coat of varnish is completely dry, the garden markers are ready for use.

WOOD MARKERS

EQUIPMENT

Carpenters saw or mitre saw
Paintbrush

MATERIALS

Lengths of approx. 65 mm (2^1/$_2$ in)
   x 12 mm (^{1}/$_2$ in) sawn softwood timber
White or light colour multi-surface
   garden paint

METHOD

1 Cut the strips of 65 mm (2^1/$_2$ in) x 12 mm
   (^{1}/$_2$ in) sawn softwood timber into lengths of
approximately 30 cm (12 in). Cut one end into
a point with a hand saw or mitre saw.

2 Apply at least two coats of multi-surface
   garden paint to all faces of the strips, paying
particular attention to the point and end grain.
When dry, a felt-tip pen or pencil can be used on
the markers. After some use, it is a simple job to
renew the finish with a further coat of paint.

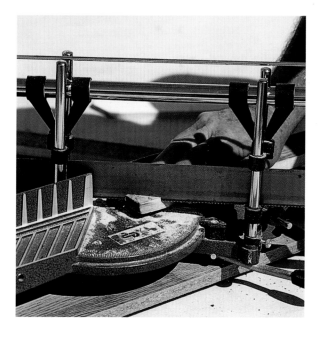

CART SHAFT FEATURE

The cart shafts used for this project were bought at auction. In the lot were also a selection of harness, some old brasses and a number of mysterious iron and wooden objects, the purposes of which we only found out later from a farmer who had spent his early life with working horses.

Made redundant by modern farming methods, much early working horse harness and tools is now rusting and rotting away on farms, a fast disappearing resource of functional artifacts largely ignored by collectors and museums which will soon be lost for all time. We used some of the metal traces and harness as decorations but the heavy shafts sat ignored for months.

When a herd of cattle almost totally destroyed our garden, the only answer was to rotavate the entire lawn and lay new turf. Three months later, we had a new lawn which stretched down to our small orchard and the open countryside beyond. We wanted to emphasise the view and decided to erect three of the shafts to frame the longest vista. Another shaft has been used as an archway leading to a garden seating area and we have plans to erect more as objets d'art.

EQUIPMENT

Paintbrush
Hammer
Sledgehammer
Spirit level
Spanner

MATERIALS

Selection cart shafts
Colourless wood preservative
Waste timber for props
Selection nails
2 metal fence spikes per shaft
Waste block of wood to fit
    inside metal spikes
Selection wooden wedges

Safety note

We advise that rubber or protective gloves are used when applying wood preservative.

CART SHAFT FEATURE

METHOD

1 Before you start constructing the feature, saturate the shafts with colourless wood preservative to treat any rot or worm and protect the timber from further deterioration. Pay particular attention to end grain and any timber that will be below the ground.

2 Nail a piece of wood to each shaft to form temporary props. Erect the shafts in the garden, moving them around until you have found the best position for each shaft. Stand back and view them from a distance, fine-tuning their positions until you have achieved the effect you want.

3 Lay the shafts on the ground just behind their proposed positions and remove the temporary props. For each shaft, use the sledgehammer cushioned by a block of wood to drive a metal fence spike for each upright into the ground. Start by driving the spike halfway, check it is upright with the spirit level, then continue to drive the spike into the ground until only its socket is visible, making sure the integral tightening bolt is still accessible.

4 You will need assistance for the final part of the job. Place the uprights of the shaft into the metal spikes and, while someone holds the shaft vertical, anchor the uprights by means of wooden wedges. Use the spirit level to check the shaft is vertical and finally tighten the integral bolt on each spike with a spanner to ensure the shaft is secure.

LOG BIRD FEEDER

EQUIPMENT

Electric drill and 32 mm (1¼ in) hole cutter
25 mm (1 in) wood chisel

MATERIALS

Wooden log
Empty metal tea light candle bases
Three 38 mm (1½ in) galvanised screw eyes
Light chain
Three small key ring or snap hooks
One large key rings or snap hook

METHOD

An old but lightweight log was selected for this project in order to make a feeder which would be large enough to hold a reasonable quantity of bird food but light enough to hang from a slight branch to discourage visits from larger birds.

1 Place the log on a flat surface and drill several holes in the top surface to make a depth of approximately 36 mm (1½ in) with the electric drill and 32 mm (1¼ in) holecutter.

2 Remove the cores of cut wood from the drilled holes with a chisel and scrape the base of the holes level.

3 Screw the three galvanised screw eyes into the extremeties of the log to provide secure anchorage points for the hanging chain. Cut the chain (salvaged if possible) into three equal lengths, join one end of each to each of the screw eyes with a small key ring or snap hook and the join the remaining ends with a larger key ring or snap hook.

4 Place an empty tea light candle base into each drilled hole in the top surface of the log and fill with a mixture of melted fat and chopped peanuts or birdseed. Leave the fat to set. Hang the bird feeder from the outer branch of a convenient tree and leave for the wild birds to discover and enjoy. Keep a number of spare empty metal tea light candle bases filled with more of the fat and seed mixture, and refill the feeder with them when the first containers have been exhausted.

Everyone welcomes birds and wildlife into their gardens. Kitchen scraps, wild bird seed, a hanging coconut and string bags full of peanuts all provide vital food for birds (and the occasional squirrel) in winter months. Large numbers of the wild bird population die over winter and garden birds can come to depend on the food put out for them. If you care for wildlife, it is a good idea to provide clean food and fresh water all year round. A regular supply of food can make all the difference to survival, particularly of fledgling birds in spring.

We enjoy watching the birdlife which surrounds our home. Three species of swan gather over winter on the fields beyond our garden, wild duck abound and the cries of curlew are a constant sound in winter. Both green and greater spotted woodpeckers are common and we keep a patch of garden wild to attract goldfinches. Recently we have seen an increasing number of buzzards but the most destructive of all our visiting birds are the myriad noisy, bullying magpies which have proliferated over recent years.

With no shortage of wood, we decided to construct a simple hanging bird feeder which would attract a cross section of the smaller species but thwart the depredations of grey squirrels and the larger jackdaws, rooks and magpies which otherwise steal the food.

WINDOW COLD FRAME

In the absence of a greenhouse, no garden should be without a cold frame, a place where plants can be started early, protected from the cold and frost. Keen gardeners, we enjoy home-grown vegetables, safe in the knowledge that they have been fed only on well-rotted farmyard manure and garden compost and are free of pesticides and sprays. Somehow they seem to taste so much better.

Unfortunately our growing season is all too short. In past years we have protected newly sown plants with glass cloches rescued from a local strawberry grower who was replacing them with plastic tunnels. The problem with cloches is that they break easily, are heavy, and are difficult to store when not in use. Luckily we had the materials from which to make a number of cold frames to replace them. For the tops we used old windows with frames and glass intact, bought at a local clearance sale. For the frames we decided to use some softwood timber planks, once used to line a roof and rescued from a local reclamation yard, just for the cost of collecting them – painted with bitumen they had so many nails in them that they were uneconomic to recycle.

Discarded windows, all too often replaced by plastic double glazing, are easy to find and should cost you little. They make a wonderful resource material and can be used as doors for wall cupboards in a kitchen, made into coffee tables, and even reused as windows in garden sheds and garages.

EQUIPMENT

Orbital sander or glasspaper
   and sanding block
Tape measure
Hand saw
Electric drill and wood bit
Electric screwdriver
Pencil or marker pen
Straight edge
Electric jigsaw
Electric planer
Paintbrush

MATERIALS

Old window frame
Quantity softwood planking
   approx. 15 cm x 25 mm (6 x 1 in)
Quantity softwood approx.
   5 x 5 cm (2 x 2 in)
Quantity 65 mm (2½ in)
   galvanised screws
Quantity softwood approx
   5 cm x 25 mm (2 x 1 in)
Length softwood approx
   25 cm x 5 cm x 25 mm (10 x 2 x 1 in)
Two metal washers
White or light-coloured opaque
   garden wood paint

WINDOW COLD FRAME

METHOD

When selecting a window frame for this project, check that the putty securing the glass in place is sound and that there are no gaps or holes which will allow moisture to penetrate the wood and encourage rot. We selected a number of window frames of equal size to make several uniform cold frames.

1 Use the orbital sander or glasspaper and a sanding block to remove any residual paint from the window frame. If the paintwork is in relatively good condition, sand it to a sound surface.

2 Measure the width of the planks you will be using for the project and decide on the height of the proposed cold frame. As the frame is designed to slope from back to front, for simplicity we used three planks for the back and two for the front. Cut two lengths of the 5 x 5 cm (2 x 2 in) softwood to approximately 25 mm (1 in) less than the combined width of two planks and two further pieces to approximately 25 mm (1 in) less than the combined width of three planks. This will give you two short and two long battens. Cut six lengths of the planking to approximately 5 cm (2 in) longer than the shorter side of the window frame to form the sides of the cold frame. Place three of the cut planks on a surface and join them together with a short batten at one end and a long batten at the other, pre-drilling the screwholes where they fall close to the ends of the planks in order to prevent the timber splitting. Repeat with the remaining three planks and two battens to form the second side piece, ensuring that when placed together the corresponding battens face each other.

3 Cut five lengths of planking each approximately 5cm (2 in) longer than the longer side of the window frame to form the front and back of the cold frame. Place three planks together on a surface and measure their combined width. These three pieces will form the back of the frame. Measure the combined width of the remaining two planks which will form the front of the frame. Take one of the assembled side pieces and mark a point at each end, the first at the height of the front of the frame and the second on the opposite end at a point approximately 1 cm (½ in) less than the height of the back of the frame. Use a pencil or marker and straight edge to draw a line from the first point to the second point and cut the side piece to shape along the marked line with a jigsaw or hand saw. Repeat with the second side piece.

4 Take the two planks cut for the frame front and pre-drill two holes at both ends of each plank approximately 25 mm (1 in) from the end, one close to the top, one close to the bottom. Fit the two planks to the sloping side pieces to form the front of the frame, screwing through the pre-drilled holes into the battens. Repeat with the three remaining planks to form the rear of the frame. The cold frame carcass is now assembled.

5 Place the assembled carcass on a level surface and use the electric plane to plane the tops of the front and back of the frame level with the slope of the side pieces. Always plane away from the ends towards the centre of the timber to minimise the risk of the planer snagging on and damaging the side pieces. Take the length of 5 cm x 25 mm (2 in x 1 in) softwood and cut to form a frame sitting on top of the carcass, the inner dimension to be just greater than the rebate size of the window and the outside to overlap the sides of the carcass. Pre-drill and fix in place with screws driven into the top of the carcass. Place the window into the rebate to check the fit. Take the piece of 25 cm x 5 cm x 25 mm (10 x 2 x 1 in) softwood timber and drill a screwhole in it approximately one third along its length. Using two washers behind the screw, attach the piece of wood to the inside of the cold frame, in the middle of the top plank at the front, to form a prop which can be used to keep the window open in order to provide ventilation for growing plants in warmer weather. The washers behind the screw will make it easier to move the prop. Finally, paint the completed cold frame with two coats of white or light-coloured opaque garden wood paint or multi-surface outdoor paint.

It is encouraging to see a growing awareness of the need to recycle and an increase in the number of people trying to do something about what we are losing. Instead of merely paying lip service to recycling and conservation, we are becoming more environmentally aware.

The decision to re-use old materials should not be driven by conscience alone. Salvaged items were often made with a commitment to quality and craftsmanship that is sadly lacking in their modern counterparts. Softwoods once used for utilitarian objects may be from species no longer harvested or cut from timber of a size not found in today's commercially forested plantations; the grain, texture and colour of many reclaimed timbers are almost impossible to find in new woods. Old hand-made bricks are difficult to replicate and the patina, shape and coloration of stone and slate that has been worn by the feet of generations is hard to emulate.

HOW TO GET IT, HOW TO DO IT

Whilst it is by no means true that all recycled materials are cheaper or more beautiful than their modern alternatives, inexpensive raw materials for re-use or conversion into new and different purposes are everywhere. Start off by looking around your home and garden and think carefully before throwing things away – there is much that can be reincarnated. Perhaps not everything we have used in this book will be available to you, but most projects can easily be adapted for use with things you find or may already own.

TOP LEFT

Two verdigris copper pyramid-topped ventilators stand in a reclamation yard ready for re-use.

TOP RIGHT

A stunning floor in the summer-house of the Lost Gardens of Heligan, carefully restored by John Nelson using as much of the original brick and stone as possible.

FAR RIGHT

An eclectic selection of architectural antiques and miscellaneous salvage lined up and labelled ready for sale at an auction held in the grounds of a country house.

HOW TO GET IT

SOURCES OF SALVAGED MATERIALS

Old metal buckets that appear to be past their usefulness can be transformed into striking garden planters. If there is too much deterioration, sink them into the soil to contain invasive plants. Corrugated-iron sheets, cut down with metal sheers or disc cutter make unusual garden edging and even a broken or battered chair becomes a rather eccentric planter! The Trellis Rack in 'Elements and Ambiance' (see page 212) is an example of how we found a different use for something that was surplus to requirements and could have easily been thrown out.

Never ignore builders' skips – a search can reveal a cornucopia of assorted things. The scaffold boards used to construct the Scaffold Bench in 'Seating and Retreating' (see page 136) were salvaged from a skip. (It is worth checking with the householder or builder that the material in the skip is intended for disposal, to avoid being accused of theft!)

You may find a building being demolished; the timbers burnt, the bricks sent to landfill and the roofing slates discarded. It is best to avoid getting in the way or holding up work, but it may be possible to make the contractor an offer for the materials you want or, better still, suggest you take them off his hands. Disposing of unwanted materials is expensive and the value of much salvaged building material can be outweighed by the cost of sorting it out.

We frequently stumble upon building sites where valuable materials are thrown away. On a recent trip we discovered a department store being gutted to make way for a new development. Shop fittings were being ripped out, panelling destroyed and hundreds of bricks dumped into a skip. After a brief word with the site foreman we were off, the boot of the car laden with bricks! An hour or so of cleaning them and we had more than enough bricks to construct the edging used for the raised garden in 'A Garden Reclaimed' see page 169).

You will be surprised by the number of old pipes found abandoned on site, too damaged for re-use but perfect for our Pipe Planter in 'Inventive Ideas' (page 222). Timber off-cuts, broken roof tiles and bricks abound, but remember, building sites are dangerous. Most have restricted access and so it is unwise to venture onto a site without authority. Always seek permission before removing anything.

Visit gardens whenever you can. Many private gardens are open to the public through

local and national garden schemes to raise funds for charity, and some have used recycled materials in inspirational ways.

Scrap-metal yards also contain a wealth of useful items. We have salvaged copper pipes to make a greenhouse sprinkler system, used scrap lead sheeting as protection for the tops of fencing posts and even adapted discarded steel reinforcing bars to construct a light and airy garden pergola. Scrap-yards can pose a danger from sharp and falling metals and so it is prudent to make your wishes known to the owner. Your finds will be weighed and you should be asked for little more than their scrap value. Car breakers' yards can be a source of inspiration too. We have seen wonderful planters constructed from old wheel hubs and were intrigued by the centrepiece in the garden of a Citroen enthusiast, who had filled an old 2CV to overflowing with flowering plants!

Scan the small advertisement column in your local newspaper for bargains. The wooden fencing in part of our garden was made from the remains of a dilapidated hen house, found as a result of answering an advertisement. Details of farm sales and auctions also appear in local papers. Farm sales are often busy social occasions where the selling of livestock and equipment accumulated, sometimes over generations, takes second place to meeting around the mobile catering van to discuss the woes of modern farming! A water trough used for the Water Feature in 'The Themed Garden' (page 192) and the cheese presses for the Cheese Press Table in 'Seating and Retreating' (page 140) were bought at farm sales. If you live in a rural area or decide to visit the countryside, chances are they will be an enjoyable hunting ground for treasure.

Car-boot sales are a godsend to the keen-eyed salvager. Whilst they have achieved

LEFT

Taps and water pipes have been welded to a brass samovar, giving this bathroom in the Bristol restaurant Byzantium a feel of the exotic East.

BELOW

Three different reclaimed doors: the one on the left is one of a pair of outer French softwood louvre doors with fretted insert, original hinges, catches and paintwork, which was preserved with several applications of tung oil. The inner door on the right is glazed with an oak frame, and behind it is a pair of double doors with their original stained glass, used to hide kitchen paraphernalia.

something of a reputation as an outlet for the disposal of goods with a dubious history, unwanted items can often be bought at bargain prices. The old paraffin lamps used for outdoor dining (see page 204) were successful purchases at a car-boot sale.

Garage sales can also be rewarding. The owners are quite likely moving and eager to dispose of household equipment, garden tools and general junk. We have bought dozens of useful terracotta pots and a collection of neglected garden tools, now displayed on the lime-washed brick wall of our rustic summerhouse.

Increasing in popularity are sales of architectural and garden antiques. Many artefacts fetch terrifically high prices but the cart and carriage shafts used in 'Inventive Ideas' (page 228) were bought at such an auction for a very modest sum. One of our most satisfying purchases was a wonderful resource of hardwood timber and mouldings.

Government surplus dealers deserve a mention. Their well-made, largely utilitarian stock, originally manufactured to exacting standards for the armed forces, is ideally suited for conversion or reuse in the home or garden. As the armed forces contract, the civil service 'downsizes' and nationalised industries are privatised, equipment is disposed of to dealers, who pass it on to the public often at very competitive prices. Ex-army ammunition boxes are perfect for storing tools and the odds and ends cluttering up most garden rooms and potting sheds. We have made an unusual garden planter from an old latrine bucket that came from a government surplus yard, as did the buckets turned into planters in 'The Themed Garden' (page 194). Another find was a number of redundant tent poles, used as the framework for an attractive garden awning.

Reclamation yards are the supermarkets of salvage, the place to find a vast resource of architectural antiques and reclaimed materials all under one roof. They offer a bewildering array of stacked timber, tiles, bricks, slates, roll-top baths, basins, panelled doors and much more besides. Do not expect knock-down prices, but sometimes dealers have difficulty in disposing of broken items or off-cuts and if you have a use for something, make them an offer. Most of the broken tiles and slates arranged as edging in 'A Garden Reclaimed' (see page 178) were found piled in a heap at a reclamation yard. On another occasion we secured a job lot of roofing timber too full of nails to be economic for the yard to remove. Although it took us time to get rid of the nails, we were able to use some of the timber to make our Potting Stand in 'Seating and Retreating' (see page 146) and the Window Cold Frame in 'Inventive Ideas' (page 234).

Some years ago enthusiasts Thornton Kay and Hazel Matravers established SALVO, the organisation that is today recognised as being the hallmark of the reliable dealer. SALVO has a worldwide membership committed to the observance of its voluntary code that is designed to promote ethical reclamation and prevent the trade in stolen artifacts or items removed from listed buildings. Their informative UK and international websites **www.salvo.co.uk** and **www.salvoweb.com** provide details of dealers in architectural antiques, reclaimed materials, antique garden ornaments, demolition companies, architects, craftsmen and numerous other professionals, listed by county or country, together with other useful addresses. 'For Sale', 'Wanted' and 'Demolitions' sections are also included.

The web is an expanding source of information. A number of local authorities and US state bodies run regularly updated web information on people and organisations both selling and looking for salvaged items. The Old House Web at **www.oldhouseweb.com** is a worthwhile site for restoration enthusiasts and offers a free email newsletter to subscribers, including useful information and contacts to would-be house renovators, albeit with an American bias. **www.recycle.net**, run by *Recycler's World*, is a materials buying and selling website. Details of other reclamation websites are provided in the 'Useful Addresses' section at the end of this book.

Travel stimulates inspiration for designs and new uses for reclamation. It also presents a chance to rescue materials that you may be lucky enough to come across. A visit to Catalonia resulted in a flight home carrying ancient olive jars as hand luggage, that were then used as decorative features in the garden. While driving through Italy we stumbled upon some pretty encaustic tiles tipped near the edge of a small wood where we stopped for our picnic. Returning from the Netherlands, we rather fortuitously fell upon a skip in Antwerp and were able to load our van with ancient handmade bricks, which we later used to make a beautiful floor.

Eastern Europe is being ravaged by foreign dealers hungry for antique furniture and decorative architectural finds whilst India and the Far East, where scant and poorly policed conservation laws go largely ignored, are next on the list for rapacious exploitation.

France remains a rich source of under-appreciated salvage. Emmaüs, a charity established to provide shelter for the homeless, has long been a resource of reclaimed materials. Whereas once cast-off clothing and items of furniture were collected and sold to fund their work, today they are a highly professional international organisation.

They are represented in most major French centres where an increasing number of trade and private purchasers beat a trail to their doors. Emmaüs, Matériaux Anciens, Dépôts Vente and Demolitions are all sources of salvage throughout France.

Wherever you locate your salvaged materials, whether searching for a particular piece or discovering something 'just too good to miss', use your imagination and think of alternative approaches for its re-use. However modest it may seem, treat it with respect – it has a history and perhaps as well as owning something unique, you will have made some small dent in the blanket of apathy which surrounds all things considered past their 'useful life'.

HOW TO DO IT

HINTS & TECHNIQUES

A number of the more common techniques used in the trade are listed on the following pages. Some you can undertake yourself, others will need to be done professionally. We have also included some essential information to read through before embarking on a project.

FIRST AID

Work involving sharp tools or power equipment entails an element of danger and a basic first-aid kit should be kept to hand in case of accidents. Familiarise yourself with the contents and keep it restocked if you have cause to use it.

SAFETY

Safety must come first. Think through the project before you start and clear the working area of any extraneous materials or equipment. Before you start a job ensure you have the correct tools, everything is in working order and take precautions to prevent unnecessary accidents. Damaged tools are dangerous and faulty power tools can be deadly. Keep them regularly maintained.

If using sharp equipment such as chisels or power saws, always work away from yourself and never cut towards, or close to, your hand or body. A moment's inattention can result in a nasty wound. Clamp anything you are cutting securely to a work surface, and use a scrap of timber to push timber through a planer or bench saw. Keep all tools, equipment and dangerous substances out of reach of children and animals.

TOXIC SUBSTANCES

Many projects involve the use of preservatives, stains and sometimes potentially dangerous substances. Read and follow the instructions on the container and make sure you have old cloths or rags to hand for wiping up spills. Never casually dispose of waste or empty containers that may cause pollution or react with other substances.

Some old timber was painted with lead-based paints. Dust from this is dangerous and it is essential that you use a dust-extraction system or a dust mask (or even full face mask) if working with these materials.

The dangers of asbestos are well known and it may be present in old buildings that are being demolished or renovated. Strict laws apply to its removal and only registered experts, properly equipped, are allowed to undertake this work. Occasionally traces of asbestos can be found on timber salvaged from old buildings. Amateurs undertaking home improvements sometimes fail to recognise asbestos and unthinkingly deposit it in a roadside skip. Err on the side of caution and, if in doubt, leave well alone.

PROTECTIVE CLOTHING

Proper protective clothing is essential. Loose clothing can become entangled in moving parts of power equipment and injuries may be caused. Always work with sleeves fastened, ties or scarves removed and long hair tied up or tucked into a hair covering.

A face or dust mask, protective gloves and overalls should be part of the workshop inventory. Eye protection is most important when using rotary sanders or other power equipment. A full face mask attached as a visor to a protective helmet is a wise investment. Obtainable from Screwfix Direct

(see 'Useful Addresses' at the back of the book), the visor is comfortable to use when operating a chain or power saw.

Protective padded clothing is also essential if you are using a chain saw and advisable if you are working with sheet metal. Head protection is a legal requirement for most building and demolition sites and you should never venture on site without wearing a helmet. Safety shoes or boots incorporating a hardened toecap and protective sole are worthwhile, as are strong rigger's or similar gloves.

ELECTRICITY OUTDOORS

Electricity is dangerous and the combination of electricity and water is potentially lethal. Never use electrical equipment outdoors if it is raining and always keep leads dry. Attach a circuit breaker to the lead of any electrical equipment used out of doors (this is essential for underwater equipment such as pumps and aerators). Should an electrical lead become damaged, replace it rather than attempt a repair.

Purpose-made electrical fittings are manufactured for outdoor use and these should only be fitted by a qualified electrician. Have all outdoor electrical installations checked by a qualified electrician before use.

TOP

When caterer Elizabeth Deacon renovated her house, a butler's pantry was created using reclaimed materials, such as the ceramic sink, taps and draining board.

BOTTOM

In this striking bedroom designed by Milo Design, the bed was constructed from wooden balcony supports cut in half to create a simple but effective look, toning well with the reclaimed floor.

Maintain your tools in good condition and store them properly. Edged tools stored where moisture is likely to affect them should be protected with a wipe or spray of oil when not is use. As far as possible, keep tools stored in a dry environment. Screws, nails and other such supplies should be kept in airtight containers. Buy most fittings as and when you need them from a company such as Screwfix Direct (see 'Useful Addresses'), obviating the need to keep large and sometimes deteriorating stocks. Tools can be hired for many projects – a cement mixer for larger jobs and a diamond rotary cutter for slicing bricks and cutting slate. The hire shop should also supply the appropriate safety equipment.

EQUIPMENT & TOOLS

Most projects in *Recycle* require only simple tools. Black and Decker (see 'Useful Addresses') supplied the tools used to assist us with this book. A well-equipped workshop should include a number of basic tools: the better the quality, the better their performance and the longer they will last.

TIMBER

Wood is the base material for many constructions and projects, and the more common woods together with some more exotic species can be found in reclamation yards. Cut, sawn and plain timber develops a colour and patina over time, adding to its appeal. Oak is a particularly attractive hardwood, but it can become discoloured by iron or steel nails or screws. Always use brass fixings in oak.

Remove old metal fixings from salvaged timber before using power equipment, as they may seriously damage your tools. All reclaimed timber should be stored in the dry and stacked to allow air to circulate around it.

PRESERVING TIMBER

Examine reclaimed timber for signs of insect infestation, fungal attack or rot and treat with a timber preservative before re-use. A number of coloured and colourless timber preservatives and finishes are available and a wood hardener can be used if parts of its structure have started to deteriorate. Timber used in contact with the ground should be saturated with preservative before use. If new timber is to be used, make sure it has been pressure treated with preservative.

STRIPPING WOOD

When removing paint or varnish from timber, several choices are available. Be aware that old paint may be lead-based and toxic – you must take every precaution to avoid inhaling dust from it. Always wear a dust mask when sanding, especially with power tools.

The first and most obvious method of paint removal is sanding, either with purpose-made tools or by hand. Sanding is time-consuming and not only is it difficult to remove paint from difficult areas, but some of the wood surface may be removed as well. Heat stripping with a heat gun and scraper used to be the usual method of paint stripping. Gas and electrical guns have replaced paraffin heat guns but these tend to scorch the wood in all but the most experienced hands.

Chemical stripping is extremely effective and particularly useful for stripping glued,

fragile or intricate objects. It is unpleasant, messy, and necessitates protective glasses and clothing, but normally has less effect on the colour of the wood than caustic stripping.

Caustic stripping should be undertaken by professionals only (see 'Pine Stripping' in most telephone directories). The results of immersion in a hot caustic-filled tank are uniformly good on most spirit-based paints, although not on water-based paints. The process imparts colour to the dipped wood, especially if the caustic has been in use for some time and can have the effect of loosening glued joints and fixings. It is not advisable to strip hardwoods in hot or cold caustic.

PAINTS, STAINS & FINISHES

Wood used outside must be protected against the weather with one of the numerous proprietary outdoor timber preservatives. Many modern garden paints contain preservative and Cuprinol (see 'Useful Addresses') make products specially formulated for garden use. Their multi-surface paints are extremely practical and give an excellent result on stone, brick, blockwork, rubber and metals, in addition to wood.

If traditional paints are being used on planed wood surfaces, the timber should be primed and undercoated before the final paint finish is applied. If wood is being varnished, use a product designed for outdoor application as interior varnishes will not withstand prolonged exposure to the elements.

Wood used indoors may benefit from any of the various colour stains, treatments or waxes currently available. Choose the colour carefully and experiment on a timber off-cut as the finish should enhance rather than mask the wood's natural grain. (For the enthusiast we recommend Frederick Oughton's book

The Complete Manual of Wood Finishing, highly informative on the finishing and treatment of wood.)

BRICKS, TILES & TERRACOTTA

Old bricks, tiles and terracotta were produced in small factories in an extraordinary variety of shapes and colours. Manufactured from local clay and distributed within a limited area, they ranged in colour from pale cream to almost black. Although in later years bricks were largely made to a standard size, they can be found glazed, unglazed, perforated, patterned or high-fired as engineering bricks for industrial use. Many bear the mark of their maker, testimony to a once-thriving industry.

Handmade bricks were produced by throwing worked clay into wooden moulds before air drying and firing. When sliced in half (using a diamond cutter) old bricks can reveal the swirling colours of the clays used in their making. Sealed with raw linseed oil or terracotta tile sealant, they make very attractive flooring. There are innumerable commercial sealants and polishes formulated specially for terracotta floors and most seem perfectly adequate. A recommendation from a supplier or a previous user is useful.

Roof tiles were produced to individual designs and reclamation yards may hold a selection of local patterns.

Old and stained bricks and terracotta can be cleaned with 'brick acid', sold by builders' merchants, or with a solution of weak hydrochloric acid. It is essential to wear gloves, protective glasses and clothing as well as a face mask. Seek professional advice before attempting cleaning – or leave it to the professionals.

Many bricks will need to have the old mortar removed, a time-consuming job requiring chipping with a bricklayer's trowel or

TOP

Stable bricks are made in a vast range of patterns and these examples were found in the yard at South West Reclamation.

BOTTOM

A weathered and worn oak sherry barrel, complete with its original stencil markings sits among a stack of wooden pallets.

bolster. A useful tip: clean old bricks covered with lime mortar by rubbing them on a concrete block. For paths and edging, bricks can be used in their original condition, but some types are susceptible to water penetration and frost damage. Engineering-grade bricks are recommended for areas exposed to severe weather conditions.

Flat roofing peg-tiles make excellent pavers for patios and are also good for wall capping. In 'Seating and Retreating' (see page 134) we show them used as the floor in a seating area and in 'Inventive Ideas' we illustrate a garden path where clay tiles have been used imaginatively. Broken tiles make very effective garden edging (see 'A Garden Reclaimed', page 178) and more mundanely, can be used as hardcore for concrete or to provide drainage in pots and planters.

Damaged terracotta pots and urns can be repaired with a two-part epoxy resin glue. A specialist, cold-setting, coloured epoxy putty – available from Milliput (see Useful Addresses) – is extremely effective for repairing and filling broken terracotta.

METALS

Salvaged metals have innumerable uses in reclamation projects for both home and garden, and a huge variety can be found in scrap-metal yards. Reinforcing rods and scaffold poles, used to construct garden pergolas and arches for climbing plants, look particularly good in an urban setting, although some welding may be necessary. Piping makes quite an unusual garden mobile and the larger copper bore pipe can be transformed into a striking curtain pole as seen in 'Rooms for Living' (page 70). Thin steel and zinc sheet may be pot-riveted to construct fashionable planters and scrap lead is extremely useful for

waterproofing gullies, roofs and capping the tops of fence posts. Stainless steel catering equipment and sink units from offices or hospitals are exciting to look at when used in an imaginative domestic interior.

Most salvaged metals show evidence of oxidation or corrosion. At best they will have tarnished or developed a patina through exposure to the elements. Some patination can be attractive, but to prevent further degradation and potential structural damage, salvaged metals should be protected with an appropriate paint or finish. A number of proprietary single-coat metal paints are available and to preserve the appearance of bright metals without them looking too brash, spraying with metal lacquer is quite effective.

AGEING METALS

It may be necessary to give new metals an impression of age, as the brashness of a replacement can spoil the look of a project or repair. Almost all metals tarnish over time; iron door furniture rusts, brass tarnishes and zinc dulls, but there are a number of commercially available 'cosmetic' treatments that can be bought in hobby and craft shops to help accelerate natural ageing, and numerous tricks of the trade that can do the same job and ensure the end result looks authentic.

ZINC

We use perforated zinc for larders made from old planks. New perforated zinc, available from most hardware stores or builders' merchants, is bright and shiny, unlike the dull, fragile zinc used on old larders. To age new zinc, dissolve copper-sulphate crystals (ordered from your chemist or pharmacist) in water and wipe the solution over the new zinc with a soft cloth or sponge. The difference will be immediately apparent.

BRASS

New brass door-furniture fittings are invaluable when the antique equivalent cannot be found. Keep a quantity of malt vinegar in a container with an airtight lid. Stripped of all lacquer, the new brass fittings can be dropped into the vinegar, left overnight and then placed in the open air for twenty-four hours. The surface of the brass discolours and the shine disappears.

STEEL

In industry and commerce vast sums of money are spent on preventing steel from rusting, while we frequently encourage it! Simply leave the steel out of doors and the weather will do the work for you. The process can be speeded up by heating the metal in a fire, then dousing it in water before leaving it for oxidation to take place. This is particularly useful for removing paint from black 'japanned' steel fittings.

CLEANING & POLISHING METALS

Some metals require ageing; with others, the opposite is true and the same material needs to be cleaned or polished. The poor condition in which many salvaged items are found may discourage all but the most enthusiastic. Old steel fittings pitted with decades of rust, copper basins turned green with verdigris and Victorian fire-places painted with layers of paint – can all be rescued and restored to something approaching their former glory.

STEEL & IRON

Paint stripper, elbow grease, wire brushes and metal polish are the standard approach to polishing metals, although a buffing machine makes short work of a laborious job. There are a number of accessories made for high-speed electric hand tools that will help, particularly when cleaning and polishing weathered and pitted iron. Cleaned and polished iron and steel can be protected with a coating of transparent furniture wax but a proprietary metal lacquer is more effective.

To give an authentic, protective, blackened appearance to wrought and cast iron, finish with stove blacking paste or grate polish (available from stove and hardware shops). This is a messy job but the result is far more attractive than paint.

BELOW

Looking through a cart shaft into a brocante in northern France, where a mouthwatering assortment of rural artefacts, bric-a-brac, salvage and antiques are offered for sale at sometimes remarkably low prices.

COPPER & BRASS

Compare modern and antique brass and you will notice a subtle difference in colour. Modern brass has more copper in its composition and professional restorers are careful to keep a stock of old brass for use when restoring antique pieces. Elbow grease and metal polish are again the prerequisites for polishing brass.

Some abrasive polishing can be undertaken with electric hand tools. Buffing brushes and compounds can be obtained from industrial finishing and jewellery suppliers.

Chefs have for years used a traditional polish made from coarse salt mixed with lemon juice or vinegar to restore their copper pans to pristine condition.

REMOVING CHROME FROM TAPS

Chrome plating can be removed by electrolysis in sulphuric acid to reveal the brass base but a simpler process is to dip the taps in hydrochloric acid, although this can result in the brass pitting. It is advisable to leave both processes to an experienced professional who will be properly equipped.

CEMENT, CONCRETE & MORTAR

Cement is the basic constituent of concrete and mortar, together with sand, gravel, ballast or aggregate. Different mixes are required for different purposes. By using commercially available bags of ready-mixed, general-purpose concrete and bricklaying mortars, you will save time and effort.
Sands and aggregates in general use:
SHARP SAND A coarse, gritty material normally used with other aggregates to make concrete.
SOFT OR BUILDERS' SAND This has finer particles and is used for bricklaying mortar.

COARSE AGGREGATE, GRAVEL OR CRUSHED STONE: With particles normally between 5 mm (¼ in) and 20 mm (¾ in), these are used to make concrete.
BALLAST OR ALL-IN AGGREGATE A mixture of coarse aggregate and sharp sand used to make concrete. Normally pre-mixed in the ratio of 2 parts coarse aggregate to 1 part sharp sand.
For most external constructions, the usual mixtures are:
BRICKLAYING MORTAR 1 part cement to 4 parts soft sand.
BLOCKWORK OR STONE MORTAR 1 part cement to 5 parts soft sand.
CONCRETE FOR DRIVEWAYS AND HEAVY LOAD AREAS 1 part cement to 2 parts sharp sand and 4 parts coarse aggregate.
CONCRETE FOR PATHS, PATIOS, BASES FOR GARDEN SHEDS AND OTHER LIGHT-LOAD AREAS 1 part cement to 3 parts sharp sand and 6 parts coarse aggregate.

Concrete foundations and paths require a sub-base of at least 75 mm (3 in) of broken stone, bricks or other rubble. If concrete is laid to a depth of less than 75 mm (3 in), a 'stronger' mixture is required.

The greater the proportion of cement used in a mixture, the 'stronger' the mix will be. 'Strong' mixes can be vulnerable to cracking if movement occurs (common in clay and some soft soils) and the addition of a quantity of lime can be advantageous. (See www.buildingconservation.com)

All the measurements are by volume – use a bucket for measuring purposes. Concrete and mortar should be mixed with a shovel on a flat surface (a sheet of waste plyboard is ideal) or in a wheelbarrow (clean thoroughly after use). Mix the dry components with the cement, continuing to mix until an even colour is achieved. Shape the mix into a mound, make a hole in the centre and add water slowly, mixing all the time until a consistency is achieved which allows you to make a series of ridges on the surface which hold their shape, using the shovel.

Newly mixed concrete and mortar should be used within two hours. It dries quite quickly but will not achieve its full strength for about seven days. Cover new work with polythene as protection from the wet and extremes of heat and cold. In very hot weather, light spraying with water once a day for a week will prevent it deteriorating. The addition of an accelerator and frost protector additives to the mixture will help drying in cold weather.

Up to the middle of the nineteenth century, before the invention of modern Portland cements, all mortars were made with lime. Various additives were traditionally used, making it easier to work, to provide better drying times and to allow some flexibility in the finished surface. Lime mortars are smoother, flexible and more durable than their modern counterparts. Ask the advice of a builder specialising in restoration or type 'lime mortar' into Google or any other search engine to find numerous informative articles on this fascinating material.

Modern masonry mortars containing up to one third limestone filler can be bought, some containing a plasticiser. Try to match the colour of existing mortar by using the local sand (or stone dust) whenever possible. Cement colouring additives are available but they should be used with caution as the mortar will change colour when dry and over time. Some old mortars contain coal ash or cinders to add colour, although industrial ash is a constituent of some modern pre-mixes.

Useful information about cement, concretes and mortars can be found on the Blue Circle Industries website, www.bluecircle.co.uk

USEFUL ADDRESSES

TOOLS & SUPPLIES

BLACK AND DECKER
210 Bath Road, Slough
Buckinghamshire, SL1 3YD
Tel: 01753 511234
Fax: 01753 551155
www.blackanddecker.com
Electrical and battery powered
hand tools for the professional
and hobbyist.

THE MILLIPUT COMPANY
Unit 8, Marian Mawr Industrial
Estate, Dolgellau, Gwynedd,
LL40 1UU
Tel/fax 01341 422562
info@milliput.com
www.milliput.com
Milliput an epoxy putty adhesive
that bonds wood, brick, cement,
metals, concrete, plastics, glass
etc. It will set under water and is
heat resistant up to 130°C.
Available in four grades:
Standard Yellow/Grey, Silver
Grey, Superfine White and
Terracotta.

SCREWFIX DIRECT
Freepost, Yeovil, Somerset,
BA22 8BF
Tel: 0500 41 41 41
Fax: 0800 056 22 56
online@screwfix.com
www.screwfix.com
Hardware and tools; plumbing
and electrical supplies by mail
order.

TIMBER TREATMENT PRODUCTS

CUPRINOL LTD
Wexham Road, Slough,
Buckinghamshire, SL2 5DS
Tel: 0870 444 11 11
www.cuprinol.co.uk
Timber treatment products,
stains and colour washes for
internal and external use.
A useful advice line for
customer queries.

ARCHITECTS, DESIGNERS AND MANUFACTURERS

ADAMS AND SUTHERLAND
Studio 1k, Highgate Business
Centre, 33 Greenwood Place,
London, NW5 1LB
Tel: 0207 267 1747
Fax: 0207 482 2359
info@adams-sutherland.co.uk
www.adams-sutherland.co.uk
Architects sympathetic to the
use of reclaimed and salvaged
materials in new buildings,
renovations and environmental
improvements.

BRAINGE LTD
Marysmere, The Meer,
Woonton Almeley,
Herefordshire, HE3 6QS
Tel: 01544 340033
info@cowparsley.com
Authors of *Recycle*; designers
and makers of furniture and
accessories using reclaimed
materials.

EDMONDS CABINET MAKERS
Buscott Farm, Station Road,
Ashcott, Bridgwater, Somerset,
TA7 9QP
Tel: 01458 210359
Fax: 01458 210096
enquiries@
edmondscabinetmakers.co.uk
www.edmondscabinetmakers.
co.uk
Cabinet makers, furniture makers
and restorers, building restoration
and designers specialising in
reclaimed materials.

LAMBIEL ASSOCIATES
Queens Studios,
117–121 Salusbury Road,
London, NW6 6RG
Tel: 020 7485 1055
lambeil@compuserve.co.uk
Architects sympathetic to and
enthusiasts for the use of
reclaimed materials.

LAVILLE FRAMES INC.
8300 Madrid Drive Suite A,
Baton Rouge, LA 70814, USA
Tel: (1) 800 561 2485

ifsales@lavilleframes.com
www.lavilleframes.com
Inventive picture frames, mirrors,
boxes, planters and accessories
all made from salvaged metal
and timber.

MILO DESIGN EUROPE LTD
28 Kings Parade Avenue,
Clifton, Bristol, BS8 2RE
Tel: 01179 741542
Fax: 07977 489941/147101
hankhankinson@hotmail.com
Property restorers and
developers. Designers of
shop, restaurant and domestic
interiors in the UK and mainland
Europe. Furniture designers.

WATSON BERTRAM & FELL
5 Gay Street, Bath, BA1 2PH
Tel: 01225 337273
Fax: 01225 448537
wbfbath@compuserve.com
www.wbf-bath.co.uk
Architects specialising in work
on listed buildings or new
buildings in conservation areas
using reclaimed materials
wherever possible.

STAINED GLASS

DECORATIVE GLASS SUPPLIED LTD
Essex Mills, Essex Street,
Bradford, West Yorkshire,
BD4 7PG
Tel: 01274 773801
Fax: 01274 773802
info@decorativeglass.co.uk
www.decorativeglasss.co.uk
Stained and decorative glass
suppliers, tools, paints and
fusing supplies.

NEIL PHILLIPS STAINED GLASS
99 Portobello Road,
London, W11 2QB
Tel: 020 7229 2113
Fax: 020 7229 1963
neil@neilphillips.co.uk
www.neilphillips.co.uk
Leading specialists in the
conservation, restoration and
sale of antique stained glass.
SALVO Code dealer.

INFORMATION ON RECLAMATION & ARCHITECTURAL ANTIQUES DEALERS & SERVICES

SALVO
10 Barley Mow Passage,
London W4 4PH
Tel: 020 8400 6222
Fax: 020 8400 6214
(UK) www.salvo.co.uk
(international)
www.salvoweb.com
First port of call for information on
reclamation dealers and items
wanted and for sale. Publishers
of information on architectural
antiques, reclamation dealers and
reclaimed building materials.
Originators of the SALVO code
and the Salvo Code Dealer list.
The invaluable SALVO website
links many different reclamation
dealers from all over Britain and
abroad.

ARTISTS AND CRAFTSPEOPLE

PAUL ANDERSON
104 West Street, Hartland,
Devon EX39 6BQ
Tel: 01237 441645
pauloanderson
@phonecoop.coop
Maker of primitive furniture
crafted from old oak and elm
joists, gates and fences which
revels in its textures, rich colours
and surface blemishes.

CANDACE BAHOUTH
The Dell, Weir Lane, Pilton,
Somerset BA4 4BF
Tel: 01749 890433
www.candacebahouth.com
Weaver, needlepoint and mosaic
artist working in reclaimed and
found materials. Author of several
books on needlepoint.

MADELEINE BOULESTEIX
2 Carlton Mansions,
387 Coldharbour Lane,
London SW9 8QD
Tel: 020 7737 8171
madbouleseix@hotmail.com

Exciting and individual handmade
electrical and candlelit
chandeliers using recycled
domestic materials.

USEFUL WEBSITES

www.architrader.com
Online facility for buying and
selling architectural salvage and
surplus building supplies.

www.bluecircle.com
Information on all aspects of the
use of modern cements.

www.bricksandbrass.co.uk
Comprehensive and simple
information for people looking for
or already owning an older house.

www.buildingconservation.com
Invaluable resource of informative
articles on all aspects of the
conservation of old buildings and
the use of traditional materials.

www.cutouts.net
Various unusual products made
from recycled materials including
coasters made from mobile
phones ands personal organisers
made from old circuit boards.

www.diydata.com
Source of information for the
do-it-yourself person and
householders. Sections on
decorating, carpentry, electrics,
general building etc.

www.ecotopia.co.uk
A good selection of recycled
glass products.

www.emmaus.org.uk &
www.emmaus-international.org
Websites detailing work of this
French originated charity, now
active internationally, providing
useful resource of second-hand,
unwanted furniture, clothing etc.

www.energywiserecycledglass.
co.uk
A lovely selection of recycled
glass products including bowls,
tiles, glasses etc.

www.freecycle.org
Grassroots non-profit movement of people who are giving and getting stuff for free in their own area. Offer your unwanted items to other people for free.

www.oldhouse.info
Issues relevant to owners of old houses.

www.oldhouseweb.com
Worthwhile site for restoration enthusiasts offering free email newsletter to subscribers, including information and contacts to would-be house renovators. Has an American bias.

www.lime.org.uk
Calch Ty-Mawr Lime's informative site providing information (and courses) on the use of lime and traditional paints.

www.recycle.net
Run by Recycler's World, a recycled materials buying and selling website

www.recycledproducts.org.uk
Directory of recycled products

www.recyclenow.org.uk
Lots of gift ideas and links to other sites.

www.recycle-more.com
One-stop recycling information centre on all aspects of salvage and recycling for the home, business or school.

www.remarkable.co.uk
A wide selection of stationery made from recycled materials.

www.scotlime.org
Specialist advice and training on the use of lime-based materials for the conservation and repair of traditional buildings.

www.selfbuildit.co.uk
Self-build site with useful list of reclamation yards, and other materials resources.

www.thelimecentre.co.uk
A source of information on the use of lime, traditional materials and hands-on courses.

www.wastewatch.org
Directory of websites providing information on the disposal and re-use of almost any material.

RECLAMATION AND ARCHITECTURAL ANTIQUES DEALERS

UNITED KINGDOM

ACE DEMOLITION & SALVAGE
Barrack Road, West Parley, Ferndown, Dorset, BH22 8UB
Tel: 01202 579222
Fax: 01202 582043
Mobile: 0589 478843
acedemo.co.uk
Reclaimed materials, timber, bricks, tiles, slates, architectural items, recycled concrete, sleepers, telegraph poles. SALVO Code dealer.

ANDY THORNTON ARCHITECTURAL ANTIQUES LTD
Victoria Mills, Stainland Road, Greetland, Halifax, West Yorkshire, HX4 8AD
Tel: 01422 377314
Fax: 01422 310372
antiques@ataa.co.uk
www.andythornton.com
Architectural antiques and decor; good quality interior woodwork, fireplaces, panelling and architectural features specialising in church interiors for the refurbishment of restaurants, pubs and hotels. SALVO Code dealer.

THE ARCHITECTURAL FORUM
312–314 Essex Road, Islington, London N1 3AU
Tel: 0207 704 0982
info@ thearchitecturalforum.com
www. thearchitecturalforum.com

Traditional reclaimed building materials including interior and exterior flooring, Georgian and Victorian chimney pieces and a selection of accessories and garden features from fountains to orangeries.

ARTISAN OAK BUILDINGS
Canterbury Road, Molash, Kent CT4 8HN
Tel: 01233 740140
Fax: 01233 740120
www.artisanoak.co.uk
Structural and decorative old oak beams and flooring. SALVO Code dealer.

AU TEMPS PERDU
30 Midland Road, St Phillips, Bristol, BS2 0JY
Tel: 0117 929 9143
www.autempsperdu.com
Architectural antiques, reclaimed building materials and restoration 'Down to earth materials at down to earth prices'. SALVO Code dealer.

BAILEYS HOME AND GARDEN
Whitecross Farm, Bridstow, Herefordshire, HR9 6JU
Tel: 01984 561931
www.baileys-home-garden.co.uk
Shop and mail order company specialising in vintage items for the home and garden.

BRONDESBURY ARCHITECTURAL LTD
Little Green Street Farm, Green Street, Chorleywood, Hertfordshire, WD3 6EA
Tel: 01923 283400
info@ brondesbury architectural.com
www. brondesburyarchitectural.com
Architectural antiques from Georgian to Edwardian periods, doors, baths, fireplaces, old radiators and heat output sheets. SALVO Code dealers.

COUNTRY BROCANTE
Fir Tree Farm, Godney, Somerset, BA5 1RZ

Tel/Fax: 01458 833052
Mobile: 07970 719708
ovel@compuserve.com
French antique country furniture, chandeliers and mirrors.

DORSET RECLAMATION
The Reclamation Yard, Cow Drove, Bere Regis, Dorset, BH20 7JZ
Tel: 01929 472200
Fax: 01929 472292
info@dorsetreclamation.co.uk
www.dorsetreclamation.co.uk
Reclaimed traditional building materials, architectural antiques, bathroom, lighting and fireplace showrooms - SALVO Code dealer.

DRUMMONDS ARCHITECTURAL ANTIQUES
The Kirkpatrick Buildings, 25 London Road, Hindhead, Surrey, GU26 6AB
Tel: 01428 609444
Fax: 01428 609445
info@drummonds-arch.co.uk
www.drummonds-arch.co.uk
Antique garden, architectural and bathroom items. SALVO Code dealer.

EASY – EDINBURGH ARCHITECTURAL SALVAGE
31 West Bowling Street, Leith, Edinburgh, EH6 5NX
Tel: 0131 554 7077
Fax: 0131 554 3070
enquiries@easy-arch-salv.co.uk
www.easy-arch-salv.co.uk
Architectural antiques, fixtures and fittings, fireplaces all under one roof. SALVO Code dealer.

ENGLISH GARDEN ANTIQUES
The White Cottage, Church Brow, Bowdon, Cheshire WA14 2SF
Tel: 0161 928 0854
Fax: 0161 929 8081
bill@english-garden-antiques.co.ukwww.english-garden-antiques.co.uk
Distinctive, unusual and often unique garden and architectural antiques

FROME RECLAMATION
Station Approach, Wallbridge, Frome, Somerset, BA11 1RE
Tel: 01373 463919
Fax: 01373 453122
info@fromerec.co.uk
www.fromerec.co.uk
Pine doors, fireplaces, slates, tiles, beams, flooring, antique stoneware, furniture, bygones etc. SALVO Code dealer.

HARPER'S BAZAAR
263 Worcester Road, Malvern, Worcestershire WR14 1AA
Tel: 01684 568 723
Fax: 01905 612837
Government surplus dealers, office and domestic furniture, garden and camping supplies.

IN-SITU MANCHESTER
Talbot Mill, 44 Ellesmere Street, Hulme, Manchester, M15 4JY
Tel: 0161 839 5525
info@insitumanchester.com
www.insitumanchester.com
Old established reclamation company dealing in salvaged garden and architectural items. SALVO Code dealer.

JAT ENVIRONMENTAL RECLAMATION
Deeside, Belluton, Pensford Hill, Pensford, Somerset, BS39 4JF
Tel: 01761 492906
jat.reclaimit@btinternet.com
Reclaimed stone, roof and ridge tiles, softwood timber, bricks and beams. SALVO Code dealer.

LASSCo
St Michaels Church, Mark Street, London , EC2A 4ER
Tel: 020 7749 9944
Fax: 020 7749 9941
st.michaels@lassco.co.uk
Also
Brunswick House, 30 Wandsworth Road, Vauxhall, London, SW8 2LG
Tel: 020 7394 2100
Fax: 020 7501 7797
brunswick@lassco.co.uk
www.brunswick@lassco.co.uk
The largest architectural salvage company with depots in

London; lighting, stained glass, chimney pieces, radiators, bathrooms, kitchens, pews, church and pub furniture oak, pine and teak flooring etc. SALVO Code dealer.

RETROUVIUS
2A Ravensworth Road, Kensal Green, London, NW10 5NR
Tel: 0208 960 6060
mail@retrouvius.com
www.retrouvius.com
Architect proprietors working with salvaged materials in contemporary settings. Bridging the gap between construction and destruction; dismantled building components for reuse in interiors and exteriors.

ROBERT MILLS RECLAMATION
Narroways Road, Eastville, Bristol, BS2 9XB
Tel: 0117 955 6542
Fax: 0117 955 8146
Specialist in gothic architectural antiques including panelling, stained glass and church fittings for pubs, restaurants and private houses. SALVO Code dealer.

RONSONS RECLAMATION AND RESTORATION
Norton Barn, Wainlodes Lane, Norton, Gloucester, GL2 9LN
Tel: 01452 731236
Fax: 01452 731888
info@ronsonsreclamation.co.uk
www.ronsonsreclamation.co.uk
Reclamation yard with vast stock of reclaimed and salvaged building materilas and artefacts. SALVO Code dealers.

SOUTH WEST RECLAMATION LTD
Wireworks Estate, Bristol Road, Bridgwater, Somerset, TA6 4AP
Tel: 01278 444 141
Fax: 01278 444 114
info@southwest-rec.co.uk
www.southwest-rec.co.uk
Reclamation dealer specialising in Bridgwater bricks and tiles, flooring and building artefacts. SALVO Code dealers.

TALISMAN
73-91 New Kings Road, London, SW6 4SQ
Tel: 020 7731 4686
Fax: 020 7731 0444
info@talismanantiques.com
www.talismanantiques.com
Architectural antiques for interiors and gardens.

WALCOT RECLAMATION LTD
Riverside Business Park, Lower Bristol Road, Bath, BA2 3PQ
Tel: 01225 335532
Fax: 01225 484317
www.walcot.com
Old-established reclamation yard specialising in architectural antiques, reclaimed building materials, bathroom fittings etc.

WELLS RECLAMATION
Coxley Wells, Somerset BA5 1RQ
Tel: 01749 677087
Fax: 01749 671089
enquiries@wellreclamation.com
www.wellsreclamation.com
Comprehensive stock of architectural antiques and reclaimed building materials.

WESTLAND & COMPANY
St Michael's Church, Leonard Street, London, EC2A 4ER
Tel: 020 739 8094
Fax: 020 729 3620
westland@westland.co.uk
www.westlandlondon.com
Antique chimney pieces, fine grates, architectural elements, paneling, paintings and furniture.

WILSONS CONSERVATION BUILDING PRODUCTS
123 Hillsborough Road, Dromore, Co Down, Northern Ireland, BT25 1QW
Tel: 0289 269 2304
Fax: 0289 269 8322
info@wilsonsyard.com
www.wilsonsyard.com
Architectural antiques and reclaimed materials. Flooring, beams and architectural items; cast iron and metalwork; clay and stone bricks, floor tiles, wall capping, setts and cobbles, flagstones etc.

IRELAND

ARCHITECTURAL ANTIQUE SALVAGE
Dromavalla, Ballyseedy, Tralee, Co Kerry
Tel: 066 718 6556
www.aasalvage.com
Fireplaces, mantels, chimneypieces, ironwork, stone troughs and planters, reclaimed brick and slate.

DECKLAD ARCHITECTURAL SALVAGE
Kingswood Cross, Naas Road, Dublin 22
Tel: 01459 5492
Fax: 01464 0089
info@architecturalsalvage.ie
www.architecturalsalvage.ie
Large stock of reclaimed materials and building supplies

EDENDERRY ARCHITECTURAL SALVAGE LTD
Monasteroris Industrial Estate, Edenderry, Co Offaly
Tel/Fax: 046 973 3156
bpmurhy@iol.ie
www.edensalvage.com
Reclaimed building materials and large selection architectural salvage and materials.

KILKENNY ARCHITECTURAL SALVAGE AND ANTIQUES
The Old Woolen Mills, Bleach Road, Kilkenny
Tel: 056 776 4434
info@eurosalve.com
www.eurosalve.com
Architectural salvage, timber, doors, windows, slate, bricks, antiques and artefacts.

LIMERICK ARCHITECTURAL SALVAGE
Castleconnell, Co. Limerick
Tel: 061 372 743
Fax: 061 372 813
www.limerickarcsal.com
Wide plank flooring, bricks, roof tiles, slates, cobbles, chimney pots, baths, basins, sandstone & limestone paving, garden statues, benches, urns, railway sleepers etc.

EUROPE

ANCIENS MATERIAUX RENOVATION DE NORMANDIE S.A.R.L.
Le Bourg, 50150 Gathemo, France.
Tel: 02 33 69 40 16
antique-french-materials.com
French timber, building salvage, stone and artefacts.

BCA ANTIQUE MATERIALS
Róute de Craon, 49500 l'Hôtellerie de Flee, France
Tel. 02 41 61 62 40
Fax. 02 41 61 23 20
Also
RN13 - 4 Avenue de Paris, 14370 Mery-Corbon, France
Tel: 02 31 23 95 87
Fax: 02 31 23 25 57
enquiries@bcl-materiauxanciens.com
bca-antiquematerials.com
Wide range of French timbers, salvaged building materials and artefacts.

HOGA COMPANY
4400-469 V.N.Gaia, Portugal
admin@hogacompany.com
www.hogacompany.com
A reliable source for antique landscape ornaments, garden antiques, old farm ornaments.

LUIJTGAARDEN BV
Kreekdijk 9, 4758 TL Standdaarbuiten, Netherlands
Tel: 0165 312 489
Fax 0165 318 136
info@luijtgaarden.nl
www.luijtgaarden.nl
Largest stock of salvaged roof tiles in Holland

THE BELGIAN SALVAGER
Gouthier SPRL, Rue de la Déportation No. 125, 7100 Haine-Saint-Paul, Belgium.
Tel: 0476 44 05 16
Fax: 064 26 42 91
pierregouthier@thebelgian salvager.com
www.thebelgiansalvager.com
Antique building materials, true to nature copies of old statuary etc. using traditional techniques.

CANADA

HAPPY HARRY'S USED BUILDING MATERIALS
1639B Cary Road, Kelowna, British Columbia, V1X 2C1 Canada
Tel: 250 862 3204
Fax: 250 862 3215
Also
HAPPY HARRY'S USED BUILDING SUPPLIES & LIQUIDATION STOCK
46 Wright Avenue, Dartmouth, Nova Scotia B3B 1G6
Tel: 902 468 2319
Fax: 902 468 3666
Also
HAPPY HARRY'S
4128 South Service Road, Burlington, Ontario L7L 4X5
Tel: 905 631 0990
Also
HAPPY HARRY'S
320 Wilsey Road, Fredericton, New Brunswick E3B 6E9
Tel: 506 454 2779
Fax: 506 459 1959
Also
HAPPY HARRY'S NEW & USED BUILDING MATERIALS
410 Mount Edward Road, Charlottetown, Prince Edward Island C1E 2A1
info@happyharry.com
www.happyharry.com
Largest recycled building materials company in Canada, yards in most states.

MIKE'S SALVAGE
2291 Rumney Road, RR#1 Midland, Ontario L4R 4K3
Tel: 705 534 1348
Fax: 705 534 1349
mikessalvage@yahoo.com
www.mikessalvage.com
Demolition contractors salvaging materials for re-use and re-sale. Electrical, plumbing, timber etc sold all from demolition work.

UNIQUITIES ARCHITECTURAL ANTIQUES
5240 - 1a Street SE, Calgary, Alberta T2H 1J1
Tel: 403 228 9221
Fax: 403 283 9226
info@uniquities-archant.com

www.uniquities-archant.com
Architectural salvage for the house and garden.

FIVE O SEVEN HOME AND GARDEN ANTIQUES
50 Carroll Street, Toronto,
Ontario M4M 3G3
Tel: 416 462 0046
Fax: 416 462 3722
info@507antiques.com
www.507antiques.com
35,000 square foot warehouse filled with fine antiques, garden furniture and a vast selection of architectural salvage sourced from Europe and the United States.

THE DOOR STORE LIMITED
1260 Castlefield Avenue,
Toronto, Ontario M6B 1G3
Tel: 416 863 1590
Fax: 416 863 5088
info@thedoorstore.ca
www.thedoorstore.ca
Decorative and functional architectural antiques salvaged from demolished buildings and houses. Mantles, stained-glass window, doors, mirrors etc.

AUSTRALIA

ADELAIDE AND RURAL SALVAGE
283 Hanson Road, Wingfield,
South Australia 5013
Tel: 08 8345 4779
Fax: 08 8347 0172
info@adelaideruralsalvage.
co.au
www.adelaideruralsalvage.
co.au
6 acres of recycled building and renovation materials, timber, floorboards, doors, windows, ply and sheet-board and interior antiques and accessories.

AUSTRALIAN ARCHITECTURAL HARDWOODS PTY LTD
PO Box 79. Kempsey, New
South Wales 2440
Tel: 02 6562 2788
Fax: 02 6562 2789
aah@midcoast.com.au
www.aahardwoods.com.au
Recycled timber for contemporary design

AUSTRALIAN SALVAGE
12 Byres Street, Newstead,
Brisbane 4006, Queensland
Tel: 07 3121 2202
Fax: 07 3252 0113
Also
#12 - 2 Danks Street, Waterloo,
Sydney 2017, New South Wales
Tel: 02 9699 1005
Fax: 02 9690 1837
sales@salvage.com.au
www.salvage.com.au
Recycles timber and building materials.

OLD RED BRICK COMPANY
165 William Street, Beverly,
South Australia 5009
Tel: 08 8347 2419
Fax: 08 8347 2144
info@oldredbrickco.com.au
www.oldredbrickco.com.au
Established 1981. Demolition contractor with vast resource of old bricks, timber, stone and other salvage including pavers, decking, doors, metalware etc.

THE BIG RED SHED
18 Summers Road, Darra,
Brisbane, Queensland 4074
Tel: 07 3279 0911
Fax: 07 3279 5612
Also
333 Kelvin Grove, Brisbane,
Queensland 4111
Tel: 07 3856 2454
sales@thebigredshed.com.au
thebigredshed.co.au
Selective timber salvage from historic structures for re-milling and resale.

THE SECOND HAND BUILDING CENTRE
432B West Botany Street,
Rockdale, New South Wales
2216
Tel: 02 9567 1322
Fax: 02 9567 1782
sales@shbc.com.au
www.shbc.co.au
Salvaged materials including timber, baths, windows, doors, stone, marble, slate, architectural antiques and artefacts.

NEW ZEALAND

DEMOLITION SUPERMARKET
28 Kioraroa Road, Whangarei
Tel: 0800 274 438
house.demolition@ igrin.co.nz
www.demo.net.nz
Buyers and sellers of building materials, fixtures, fittings and unique items sourced from demolished and refitted homes and buildings.

JACOB DEMOLITION AND BUILDING SUPPLIES LTD
33 Creek Street, Drury,
Papakura, Auckland
Tel: 09 294 7472
Fax: 09 412 9460
winjacob@jacobdbs.co.nz
www.jacobdbsco.nz
Buyers and sellers of a wide range of new and recycled building and landscaping materials, process and cut timber and give professional building and renovation advice.

NO NAME BUILDING RECYCLERS
3 Glover Street, Ngauranga,
Wellington
Tel: 04 499 4449
Fax: 04 499 4447
www.noname.co.nz
Reclaimed timbers and building materials.

THE PUMPHOUSE DEMOLITION YARD
Corner Tuam Street &
Mathesons Road, PO Box 32,
137 Christchurch
Tel: 033 389 6638
Fax: 03 389 6695
www.thepumphoues.co.nz
Commercial, industrial and residential demolition contractors specialising in recovery of salvageable materials.

SOUTHERN DEMOLITION
29 Mowbray Street, Waltham,
Christchurch
Tel: 03 365 9164
eddie@southerndemolition.
co.nz

www.southerndemolition.
co.nz
Re-machined salvaged native and imported timbers, bricks, steel, doors and windows.

INDEX

ACKNOWLEDGEMENTS

Our thanks to all at Kyle Cathie Publishers: **Kyle Cathie, Caroline Taggart, Dominic Brendon** and **Fiona St George**, our photographer **Tim Winter** and his assistant **Jo Fairclough**.

Our thanks also to the companies who generously helped us with equipment, materials and advice:

Black and Decker
Hand and power tools for the professional and handyman.

Cuprinol Ltd
Timber treatment products, and decorative colour stains and finishes.

Screwfix Direct
Hardware and tools by mail order – overnight.

Also to all those who kindly allowed us to photograph their homes, gardens and business premises:

Susan Boss and **Tony Hill**
Angela Coombes and **Michael Hewitt**
Leo and **Jilly Cooper**
Mr and **Mrs Hubert Fear**
Peter and **Sarah Fineman**
Ron and **Judy Mathews**
Alan and **Lucy Moore**
Peter and **Justine Morris**
Mike Nelhams and **Andrew Lawson**, Tresco Abbey Gardens
Peter Watson and **Jacqui Spencer**
Richard Wallace and **Corrina Sargood**
John Teller and the Ashley Vale Allotments Association
Joe and **Angela Tucker**
John Woolley
Mike Duckett, Lands End Nurseries
Mark Durston-Sweet, Blakeway Fisheries
Ben Pike, Bluestone Water Features
Sandra Spearing: South West Reclamation
Thornton Kay and **Hazel Maltravers:** SALVO
Hank and **Sophia Terry:** MILO Design Europe Ltd

Elizabeth and **Crispin Deacon**
Saltmoor House,
Saltmoor,
Burrowbridge,
Somerset TA7 0RL
Tel. 01823 698092
Caterers, who also offer a prestigious Bed and Breakfast service

Arne Ringner proprietor Byzantium restaurant,
2 Portwall Lane, Bristol, BS1 6NB.
Tel. 0117 922 1883
Fax. 0117 922 1886
email: info@byzantium.co.uk website
www:.byzantium.co.uk

Charlton House Hotel
Shepton Mallet,
Somerset BA4 4PR
Tel. 01749 342008,
Fax. 01749 346362,
email: reservations-charltonhouse@btinternet.com,
website: www.mulberry-england.co.uk

John Nelson and **Tim Smit**
The Lost Gardens of Heligan
Pentewan, St Austell
Cornwall PL26 6EN
Tel: 01726 845100
Fax: 01726 845101
email: info@heligan.com
website: www.heligan.com

Robert Dorrien-Smith
The Tresco Estate
Tresco, Isles of Scilly
Cornwall TR24 0QQ
Tel: 01720 422849
Fax: 01720 422807
email: contactus@tresco.co.uk
website: www.tresco.co.uk
Tresco Abbey Gardens, The Island Hotel, The New Inn, Hell Bay Hotel (Bryher), Timeshare and holiday rental properties.

Ron and **Yvonne Sargent** and **John Haynes**
The Bone Cave
Banwell
North Somerset
Tel/Fax: 01934 820516
The bone cave, stalactite cave, Banwell Tower and the follies.

Nigel and **Rosalie Dawes**
Birtsmorton Court
Nr Malvern
Worcestershire WR13 6JS
Tel: 01684 833888
Fax: 01684 833837
email: enquiries@birtsmortoncourt.com
website: www.birtsmortoncourt.com
Corporate hospitality and wedding venue in their mediaeval moated manor house.

Sarah Giddens
Giddens Landscape Design and Management
12 Castle Street
Hereford HR1 2NL
Tel: 01432 358031
email: info@gldm.co.uk
website: www.gldm.co.uk
Landscape design specialising in period and historic gardens. Sport and recreation facility design.

Thanks also to Clive and Alex Limpkin for their garden props and to all the following people whose addresses can be found in our 'Useful Addresses' section.

Candace Bahouth: mosaic artist; **Pete Chapman** and **Jeff Blagdon**: Au Temps Perdu; **Haydn Davies**: Wells Reclamation; **Sarah Mansfield**: Edmonds Cabinet Makers; **Lawrence Harper**: Harper's Bazaar; **Steve Horler**: Frome Reclamation; **Thornton Kay** and **Hazel Maltravers**: SALVO; **Robert Mills**: Robert Mills Reclamation; **Tim** and **Nicky Ovel**: Country Brocante; **Hank** and **Sophia Terry**: Milo Design; **John Tyler**: JAT Environmental Reclamation; **Sandra Spearing**: South West Reclamation; **Mark Watson** of Watson Bertram and Fell: architects